West Country Coroner

The Notable Cases and Absorbing Career of North Devon's Coroner

Brian Hall-Tomkin
with Brian Hilliard

COUNTRYSIDE BOOKS
NEWBURY, BERKSHIRE

First published 1999
© Brian Hall-Tomkin and Brian Hilliard 1999

COUNTRYSIDE BOOKS
3 Catherine Road
Newbury, Berkshire

ISBN 1 85306 596 X

Designed by Graham Whiteman

Produced through MRM Associates Ltd., Reading
Printed by J. W. Arrowsmith Ltd., Bristol

CONTENTS

Foreword

All the incidents in this book are based on facts made public at inquests in Devon where I was a Coroner for over 30 years. Inquests are confined to establishing who died, when and how and where the death occurred: they do not apportion blame, nor can they name individuals who might in any way be responsible for the death around which the inquest is held. The public and press are always admitted to inquests (other than those involving a matter of national security) and the press can, and does, comment on issues connected to the death which have nothing to do with the inquest.

The additional material in this book which was not required for the limited purpose of the various inquests has been obtained by Brian Hilliard from media reports and from individuals with a firsthand knowledge of specific cases.

We have, however, changed the names of some individuals involved in these inquests, and have also changed some locations, or left them unspecified. This has been done to avoid unnecessary grief to surviving relatives and friends, although, in almost every case the deaths have been the subject of local, national, and sometimes international, newspaper reports.

One of the unwritten responsibilities of a Coroner is to ease the suffering caused to relatives by the death of a loved one. We hope that this book will help those who have not had to deal with the 'violent or unnatural death' of a friend or relative to understand the trauma caused by such deaths, and to help them should they be faced with a similar situation in the future.

Brian Hall-Tomkin

Brian Hall-Tomkin

1

The Role of the Coroner

In the 1940s and 1950s, small boys dreamed of becoming engine drivers, fighter pilots, Test cricketers, even police officers. I cannot remember entertaining any of these worthy ambitions. Certainly no one I knew ever expressed a wish to be a Coroner when they grew up; in fact, I doubt if my contemporaries had even heard of the office. I had been born in the house in which, a century before, the Reverend Sabine Baring Gould, the composer of *Onward Christian Soldiers* had been born, but this had not inspired me to become a clergyman. During the war, I was evacuated to Canada, but returned with no wish to be a wheat farmer. Part of the journey back was by a Catalina Flying Boat, a mode of travel which perhaps dampened any enthusiasm I might have had for a career on the sea or in the air.

No, I was destined to be a doctor. My father was a doctor, I went to Epsom College, a school founded for the sons of doctors, and at the age of 18 I went to Cambridge to read Natural Sciences, as a preliminary to becoming a doctor. My future had been decided, and I was quite happy to go along with my parents' wishes. But two minor events altered that future.

While at Epsom, I had been introduced to the sport of smallbore rifle shooting, and joined the University team, which, I'm happy to report, beat Oxford in each of the three years during which I was a member. However, my devotion to competitive shooting far outweighed my devotion to my studies, and this lack of application, combined with a growing disenchantment with the newly founded National Health Service, ended my medical career before it had begun.

The disenchantment can be illustrated by one episode, which now sounds apocryphal, but which, my father assured me, was a true mirror of the time. A woman patient attended the surgery of my father's assistant and demanded a prescription for a large amount of cotton wool. 'Demanded' is the right word. In the early 1950s, there was still much debate about the manner in which the NHS was to operate, and many patients were encouraged in the belief that theirs was the right to tell a doctor what was wrong with them and what the treatment should be. Anyway, the cotton wool lady felt no obligation to tell her doctor why she wanted so much cotton wool, or what she had done with two previous, equally large, prescriptions. My father heard later, from the surgery cleaner, that the woman had proudly told her neighbours that she had used the cotton wool to stuff the arm of an ailing sofa.

To my very experienced father, and to my completely inexperienced self, this was not our idea of practising medicine, and we decided that the law was an equally honourable vocation. I was therefore articled to an Exeter solicitor, who, fortunately, was also a keen rifle shot who had captained the English rifle team. My legal studies were completed with more enthusiasm than I had devoted to medicine, and in 1959 I qualified as a solicitor and two years later joined the Bideford practice in which I still work. The senior partner in the firm was the local Coroner, the first holder of that office I had ever met, and so I learned the duties and responsibilities of the Coroner almost by osmosis.

Basically, a Coroner investigates sudden or unexplained deaths, and holders of the office must be medically

Barnstaple Council Chamber, also used as a Coroner's Court.

qualified doctors, barristers, or solicitors of at least five years' standing. In 1964 I was invited to become the local Deputy Coroner, and continued to learn through the 'sitting by Nelly' approach. 'Sitting by Nelly', a training method in which the pupil watches what the teacher does before being allowed to attempt the task himself, is not to be despised, providing that the teacher knows what he is doing. Today, Coroners have much more professional training through the Home Office, the Coroners' Society, and regional societies.

My Coroner retired at the end of 1966 and, on 1st January 1967, I was appointed as Her Majesty's Coroner for North Devon. At 32, I was the youngest Coroner in the country. Within five years my area had been merged with Barnstaple, and then with West Devon to form, geographically, the largest Coroner's district in England and Wales.

My first inquest case came as a very newly appointed Deputy Coroner. I was telephoned during a local Round Table meeting one evening by a young and anxious police sergeant. A lady who had been walking with her husband on a seaside coastal path was found dead on the beach below. My mind started racing – did she slip? – did she jump? – was she pushed? – was it a murder? And most importantly, what do I do now? Having expressed my concerns to the sergeant, I was greatly relieved to find that he was in a similar position: it was the first sudden death that he had dealt with. Between us justice was done and a verdict of accidental death was recorded.

Some cases, by their nature, are more tragic than others (although each is as distressing to the people immediately involved), especially those involving the deaths of young children, or the now increasingly fewer cot deaths. Those which are particularly unsettling involve situations where a fatal accident could have been so easily avoided – perhaps by a parent holding a child's hand to prevent it running into the road. One has to resist the instinct to pass some comment at the inquest – 'What a pity mummy didn't hold little Johnnie's hand'. Such a remark is very likely to produce tomorrow's headline: 'Coroner pillories grieving parent'.

It is easy, as in so many walks of life, to not fully appreciate the impact of what you say upon your listener. Early in my career before the appointment of full time coroner's officers it was necessary to leave my telephone number at the local police station if I was to be away from home out of normal office hours. This resulted in being rung at 9 pm on a Saturday night whilst at a party in someone else's home. The hostess called me to the telephone. Having dealt with this new fatality I almost casually remarked to her, half as an apology for interrupting the party and half jokingly, 'What an inconvenient time to die' and thought no more about the incident.

Some two years later I was chatting to a local GP who, when he heard my name, became unusually interested.

'Brian Hall-Tomkin, the Coroner?'

'Yes, that's right.'

'Do you know a Mrs Robinson? She's about 40 or so, lives in The Crescent?'

'Yes. I've been to a number of parties at her house.'

'Well, I'm telling you this in professional confidence. I've just pumped out her stomach because she took an overdose of tablets and the first thing she said to me on recovering consciousness was: "Hello doctor, I stopped taking the tablets because I realised it was evening and Brian Hall-Tomkin doesn't like being disturbed out of office hours." '

Whatever the cause of her overdose might have been, the story had a happy ending. She made a full recovery, and went on to do much good work among the elderly in the community before dying many years later of natural causes. It is not often that one is given the privilege (however unwittingly) of saving someone's life by a chance remark!

In my early days the general attitude of the families and friends who attended inquests was naturally one of distress and sadness, but tinged with some appreciation for what had been done to try and minimise the trauma of the situation and to assist in expediting funeral arrangements, registration of death, and other procedures. Today, however, whilst occasionally this is still the case it is quite common to hear remarks indicative of our increasingly materialistic society. Almost always, after the conclusion of an inquest on a road traffic fatality, someone will ask, 'Well, is that it? Who is going to pay then?'

Apart from the obvious failure to appreciate the purpose

of the inquest, it is a sad reflection on modern society's wish to deal with death by reducing it to monetary terms.

Although about one in three of all deaths in the country is reported to the Coroner, and about one in every six or seven deaths so reported requires an inquest, the Coroner's function is still not well understood, so allow me to give you a step by step account of his role.

The simplest cases involve the deaths of those who have not been attended by their medical practitioners 'in their last illness'. This phrase is usually accepted as covering approximately the last 14 days of life, and is used where an elderly patient with a medical history of having had, perhaps, a series of heart attacks, and who has seen the doctor infrequently, is found dead in bed or sitting in a chair in the lounge.

In these cases the doctor telephones the Coroner to discuss the case. If the Coroner is satisfied that the death is a natural one, with no suspicious circumstances, and the general practitioner can give a specific cause of death, then the doctor will issue a certificate and the Coroner will issue a form (known as a Pink A) in support, allowing the Registrar of Deaths to record the death. The resultant death certificate will not indicate that the Coroner has been involved.

When the medical cause of death is not known or is uncertain, the body will be taken to the mortuary at the local hospital where a post-mortem examination will be carried out by a local pathologist. This examination may include tests for blood and urine alcohol levels and, sometimes, for the presence of various drugs.

If the post-mortem result shows a natural cause of death and the circumstances are otherwise unremarkable then the Coroner issues a form to the Registrar (known as a Pink B) who will register the death and issue the certificate. Such a certificate will indicate the post-mortem findings and the involvement of the Coroner. When the body is to be cremated the Coroner issues the appropriate form (known as a Certificate E) but if there is to be a burial the Registrar will deal with the paperwork involved.

When a death cannot be dealt with by the Pink A or Pink B procedure, an inquest will be held and this is perhaps the most misunderstood aspect of the Coroner's work.

An inquest is not a trial to apportion blame for someone's death; it is a fact finding exercise to establish:
- who the person was (which is not always obvious)
- how, when and where the death occurred.

Following this, the Coroner has to record a verdict. This might be that the subject died of natural causes, industrial disease, dependence on, or abuse of, drugs, through want of attention at birth, suicide, attempted abortion, accident, lawful or unlawful killing. Where a cause cannot be properly decided the Coroner may return an Open Verdict.

Relatively few deaths require inquests to be held with a jury, and they are mostly deaths that occur in police custody or in prison. However, the Coroner has some discretion to summon a jury if it is thought appropriate.

A sudden or unexpected death naturally brings distress to close relatives, and for this reason, the initial investigation to establish the identity of the deceased, the main circumstances of the death and the post-mortem examination itself is dealt with as quickly as possible. An inquest is opened for this evidence to be given (usually by the coroner's officer) and then adjourned so that the circumstances can be fully investigated and all the evidence for a full inquest can be obtained. This will enable the Coroner to sign a Certificate for Cremation or an Order for Burial, as appropriate, and thus not delay any funeral arrangements which a family may wish to make. Following the opening and adjournment of the inquest, inquiries continue, usually conducted by the coroner's officer.

Occasionally there is a problem over who is entitled to the certificate. A man may have been married twice, for instance, and a dispute might develop between the former wife and the widow as to who will arrange the details of the funeral. Sometimes I find it prudent to deliver the certificate to the funeral director and to then retire gracefully from the scene. When a solution cannot be agreed, the matter may have to be settled by the court.

Let us consider a fairly common inquest, of the type held into the death of a driver in an accident involving two cars.

Among the witnesses may be the police officers who took measurements at the scene, the plan drawer who prepared a sketch from those measurements, the photographer who took pictures of the crashed vehicles and marks on the road at the scene. There may be vehicle examiners to report on the crashed vehicles, another police officer who is an expert in accident reconstruction, and the pathologist who carried out the post-mortem examination, although the latter is rarely called to give evidence in person.

In examining these and other witnesses, the Coroner tries to minimise the grief that might be caused to relatives and friends who have attended the inquest. Post-mortem findings, for instance, are usually non-controversial albeit they might list a series of injuries, including broken bones and damaged organs, usually collectively referred to as 'multiple injuries', but there is no need to detail them unnecessarily. Often only the basic cause of death is made public. However, a written copy of the full post-mortem report is sent to the deceased's general practitioner so that the family can have a private consultation if they wish to have more detail. It is understandable that a family would want to know if the deceased died instantly or whether there was any suffering.

Samples are taken from anyone killed in a road traffic

accident who is over 16 years of age and who dies within twelve hours of the incident, to investigate the possible presence of alcohol in the blood and urine. This information, with other particulars such as the relevant speed limit and time of day or night, is eventually forwarded to the Transport Research Laboratory to help to provide national statistics for future use.

There have been instances in which families have objected to a post-mortem examination being carried out on religious grounds or on the basis that 'the deceased has suffered enough' or 'you're not going to have him cut up any more', but Coroners have the right to order a post-mortem which they consider will provide valuable evidence for the inquest. (There was a case, some years ago, in which the father of a twelve year old boy, killed in a traffic accident, went to the hospital and took his son's body home in order that the family could pray and mourn around the corpse. With some reluctance, he agreed to release the body in order that a post-mortem could be carried out, but only on the condition that it be returned to him after the examination.)

It is essential to know the precise cause of death since, for example, a deceased car driver may have had a heart attack and died of natural causes before the accident which apparently was the cause of death. This naturally will affect life insurance claims, particularly where a company is committed to pay double on accidental deaths. This point was well illustrated in a case of mine when a moped rider was found in a ditch on the outside of a bend in the road with a fractured skull after having struck a tree. The post-mortem findings indicated that a brain haemorrhage had occurred before the accident itself, so the unfortunate rider was dead before the accident occurred and the injury to the skull was not relevant. In a similar case in which a builder had fallen from a roof, it was found that he had suffered a heart attack and was dead before he fell.

The witnesses required for the inquest will be interviewed by the Coroner's Officer or his police colleagues. In many cases, the witness statements already provided to the police in respect of the incident can be used. In the example of the fatal accident, the occupants of both cars and independent witnesses such as other drivers and pedestrians will be interviewed. I am still amazed at the difference in the accounts of the same incident that eyewitnesses provide, particularly when it comes to estimating speed.

When all the evidence has been gathered the adjourned inquest takes place. This can be as traumatic for relatives or friends as the funeral and is conducted with as much informality and sympathy as possible. One way of alleviating the trauma is for the Coroner, or the Coroner's Officer, with the permission of the witness, to read out the witness's statement, but questions may still be put to the witness by the Coroner or by the representatives of 'any interested party'.

The last witness to be called is usually the Coroner's Officer whose evidence is really a précis of that which has already been heard. It is usual, at this point, for the medical cause of death to be given together with blood/urine, alcohol or drug levels. It is also at this stage that the existence of a suicide letter, but not its contents, may be made public. The Coroner's Officer will hand it to the Coroner saying, 'The deceased left a letter indicating that he intended to take his own life.' Relatives are entitled to a copy of the letter, but, strictly, not to the letter itself, even if it was addressed specifically to them. Naturally, where the letter itself is of sentimental importance to the relatives, the rule can be waived.

If there is a jury, the Coroner must sum up the evidence

and indicate the range of possible verdicts; in non jury cases he will sum up only if he thinks it necessary. In either case the inquest is concluded with the announcement of the Coroner's, or of the jury's, verdict. If anyone is not satisfied with the result or conduct of an inquest there is a right of appeal to the High Court, for example, to have the verdict quashed and an order made for a new inquest to be held by a different Coroner.

One of the greatest plus-points of being a Coroner, I have found, is to have the privilege of being offered the opportunity to try and alleviate pain and suffering by dealing with situations in as sympathetic a manner as each case allows. One sees people, usually for the first and only time, at perhaps the lowest emotional point in their lives. I never fail to be amazed at the resilience of the human spirit. Many people suffer terribly, but seem to be able to bounce back to normality; though one wonders at the psychological cost.

Another bonus of the office is that having been conditioned to deal with death on a daily basis, everyday problems can be kept in their proper perspective. It may be that having been brought up in a doctor's family, coupled with three years as a medical student, I have become conditioned to death in all its forms, while my training as a solicitor has helped to engender a sense of logic and objectivity which in turn equips me to withstand the pressures involved.

If I had to list the three most important rules for a Coroner they would be: first, carefully consider the facts; second, do whatever is necessary; third, go to bed and sleep. It is no good lying awake at three o'clock in the morning wondering if at 10 am the day before you should have handled a case in a different way. If one is a worrier by nature and can't let go, then a Coroner's life is not going to be a happy one.

It is essential to preserve one's sense of humour if one is to keep the most stressful of situations in perspective. In 1985, at the relatively early age of 51 years, I had a heart attack and was taken by ambulance to the Intensive Care Unit at the local hospital. On the journey the ambulance attendant leaned over me (strapped on a stretcher) and solicitously enquired if I had ever been to hospital before.

Realising this was far too good an opportunity to miss I replied, 'Yes, but always to the mortuary because I'm the Coroner.' This produced 15 seconds of silence followed by, 'Well, that stops the conversation, doesn't it?'

There was a further short pause and the attendant then tapped the driver on the shoulder and related the conversation to him. This produced a nervous twitch of the steering wheel and a dramatic reduction in the speed of the ambulance.

However, the last laugh was on me for at the conclusion of the return journey to my home some ten days later the ambulance driver, having deposited me carefully in an armchair, looked over his shoulder as he left the room and said, 'Look after yourself. We don't give Green Shield stamps on the second trip!' (An interesting insight as to how he deals with the stress of his job.)

The final consideration is to be found in the best book in all the world, in the Old Testament, and I quote from Chapter 3 of Proverbs verses 5-8 (Good News Bible). The passage is appropriately headed 'Advice to Young Men':
'Trust in the LORD with all your heart. Never rely on what you think you know. Remember the LORD in everything you do, and he will show you the right way. Never let yourself think that you are wiser than you are; simply obey the LORD and refuse to do wrong. If you do, it will be like good medicine, healing your wounds and easing your pains.'

2

Treasure Trove

The Coroner has another duty, which is to hold inquests on items which might be treasure trove (treasure found buried). This function is left over from medieval times when such items became the property of the Crown. There are perhaps no more than 25 such inquests in a year in England and Wales, and there are 144 Coroners.

For centuries, until new regulations came into force in 1997, for an item to be treated as treasure trove it had to consist of a substantial amount of gold or silver. It must also have been intentionally hidden, with the idea of being repossessed at some future date either by the owner or his heirs who can no longer be identified.

The Coroner will make enquiries about the circumstances in which the find was made. Statements will be taken as for any other inquest, and the basic format of the inquest will be similar to the normal inquest with the subject matter being a metal object or objects as opposed to a body. The inquest always then had to be held before a jury which would determine the essential facts. If the jury's verdict was a finding of treasure trove the item or items were then sent to the British Museum, their worth assessed and a reward paid to the finder. Over the years I have held two such inquests and I have had two 'near misses'.

The first of the latter was a number of coins found by using a metal detector on a beach in North Devon. It appeared likely that they were part of the wages for the crew from a Royal Naval vessel which had foundered off the coast some two centuries previously. The find was duly reported and the coins were deposited at Ilfracombe Police Station.

Not being absolutely sure of the procedures, I was about to start to research the subject in one of the standard textbooks on Coroners when I had a telephone call from the Receiver of Wrecks, an office which the early Coroners had also tried to take over. The gentleman on the other end of the phone, in the politest possible way, asked if I was aware that the coins had been found on a part of the beach that lay below the High Water Line. I told him that I had not yet read the papers thoroughly, but I had no reason to doubt him. Anything found below the High Water Line is the Receiver's responsibility, so the coins went off to him.

The other case involved a set of early Georgian silver coins which had been found in a container in the wall of an old church in one of the local villages during a refurbishment. It was established that the custom of putting coins in buildings for later discovery was quite widespread. Even today, masons will put a new penny under the foundation stone of a new building. So I had to abandon my hopes of holding this rare form of inquest. The coins were replaced to be found by someone else at the next refurbishment.

However, following the introduction of the Treasure Act 1996 – its provisions came into force in 1997 – there were two main changes to what we now know as Treasure. First, the nature of the items to be considered has been substantially extended to include artefacts such as pottery, weapons, perhaps even manuscripts, and secondly, the requirement to hold an inquest with a jury has been abolished. As a result there is likely to be a marked increase in the number of inquests into Treasure.

3

From Here to Australia

As I said in my introduction, the scope of any inquest is very limited. The Coroner has to determine who died, when the death occurred, and what was the cause of death? It is no part of the Coroner's function to apportion blame, even when the deceased has been killed, and even if the identity of the killer is suspected.

Valerie Crompton was a part-time teacher at a local school. She was in her late fifties, preferred flowing dresses to trouser suits, was well liked by her colleagues and pupils, and had been a married man's mistress for 20 years. The affair was known, even to her lover's wife who, reluctantly, tolerated it. Nevertheless, Valerie continued to command the respect of her neighbours and her colleagues who valued her conscientious approach to her work; so conscientious that when she failed to ring the school after reporting herself sick, two of her fellow teachers became genuinely worried. She had phoned the school on Monday and said that if she was still unwell on Tuesday, she would let them know. Tuesday passed without anyone hearing from her, and there was still no message on Wednesday, and no reply to phone calls to her cottage. This was so unusual that two of her colleagues called at her cottage to see if she wanted any help.

Valerie lived on a small holding with a stable for her horse, and a field in which she kept a handful of sheep. The two teachers could get no answer to knocks and rings at the front door, and could see no sign of Valerie when they looked through the ground floor windows. Her horse was still in its stable and was clearly restless; the feed box was empty, and the straw dirty. The two teachers rang the local police and were able to convince them that Valerie's absence was most unusual. Two officers came to the house and broke in. There was no sign of Valerie, no sign of any disturbance, but there were some indications – a half empty wardrobe, a cleared dressing table – that she had packed and gone away.

Was there anyone else who might know where she could be? Well, it was fairly common knowledge, the teachers told the police, that Valerie was a very good friend of the Harrises who lived about 15 miles away. In particular, she was a good friend of the husband, Clifford Harris. The Harrises would know where she was. The sergeant at South Molton police station knew the Harrises' daughter, Pam Lock and her husband, John, who lived in the area. He phoned her to ask if she had any idea of how he could contact her parents?

'Oh, Mum and Dad? They're in Australia. They flew out there yesterday. They arranged the trip ages ago. Why do you want to talk to them?'

'Well, it's slightly awkward. There's a friend of theirs, Valerie Crompton. She hasn't been into work, and she's not at home. We just wonder where she might be. Your parents might know. We've been told that Mr Harris is a very good friend of Valerie's.'

Pam gave them the address at which her parents were staying in Australia, and if she thought it strange that the police should ask her not to mention anything about this conversation should she happen to speak to her parents within the next few days, she said nothing about it. It is fair to say that Mr Harris was not well liked by his immediate family. Pam did, however, mention the conversation to her husband John when he came in from working on their small holding in the evening.

'Wonder if she's in the back of your father's truck?' he said, lightheartedly. 'I'll have a look at it tomorrow. Haven't really been happy about it since your Dad left it in the field.' On their way to the airport to catch the flight to Australia, Mr and Mrs Harris, driving in two separate cars – their relationship appears to have been such that if they ever had to go anywhere together they always travelled separately – had called at the house. Clifford wanted to leave his Toyota truck with them while he was away in Australia.

'Stick it in the yard,' John told him.

'No, it's full of old muck and all smelly,' said Clifford. 'I'll leave it at the top of the field, out of your way.' He turned down John's offer to clean the truck out for him. He was quite decisive about it.

'No, don't you touch it at any price. I'll just leave it, and pick it up when I get back.'

He drove the Toyota into a field, leaving it as far as possible from his son-in-law's house. Then, he came back from the field, got into his wife's car and drove off with her to the local rail station to catch a train to Heathrow. Beyond noticing that the truck had a couple of beehives on top of the other rubbish in the back, John had thought nothing further about it, until Pam told him of Valerie's disappearance. Early the next morning – he was to lead a local shoot at nine – he went back to the truck.

John's phobia about bees was well known. It seemed to him that the beehives on the back of the truck had been deliberately placed there to prevent him looking at the rest of the contents. Well, it was winter, there were no signs of bees about, and John was convinced that there was something more than concern for him that had made Clifford park the truck so far from the house.

There were more broken beehives, old timber, and bags of rubbish in the back of the Toyota. There was also a roll of old carpet, quite bulky, wrapped in plastic and tied tightly with twine. John felt the long parcel. There was something round in the centre. It was too securely tied to unfasten easily, so he went back to the house and found a knife. He slit the parcel at the bottom, and saw, as something at the back of his brain had told him he would see, two feet protruding from the inside of the carpet. He went back to the house and called the police. The body was, of course, that of Valerie Crompton. Later that day, a pathologist established that she had been hit in the face and that the back of her skull was fractured, which could have been as the result of falling backwards after the blow had been struck.

There was an immediate suspect, Clifford Harris. It did not take long for police to discover that his affair with Valerie was common knowledge locally, and his attempts to keep his son-in-law from searching the back of his truck indicated that he was well aware that it contained Valerie's body. Police notified their colleagues in Perth, Western Australia, of Harris's presence in that city, obtained a warrant for his arrest, and began proceedings to obtain an extradition warrant. The Australian Federal Police and Western Australian Police agreed to trace Harris and to keep him under a 24 hour surveillance until the extradition warrant had been granted. In the meantime, Devon and Cornwall officers began inquiries into Clifford Harris's background.

First of all, was Margaret Harris involved? They soon decided that this was most unlikely. The Harrises had been leading separate lives for many years. Mr Harris had once, it was said, slapped his wife across the face. Mrs Harris, a well built woman, hit him back immediately with such force that he was knocked to the ground. He never again

Clifford Harris left his truck at his son-in-law's, with instructions that it was not to be touched. (*North Devon Journal*)

raised his hand to her, but the incident could have done little to heal the undisguised rift in their relationship. Besides, there was the longstanding affair with Valerie Crompton.

The affair with Valerie Crompton had been going on for 20 years. Margaret Harris, Clifford Harris, and Valerie Crompton had all once been teachers; Clifford and Valerie had taught at the same school. When Valerie married a squadron leader in the Royal Air Force, Clifford had acted as best man. He had then given up his post as a teacher and started work as a carpenter. Some of his first jobs had been at the Cromptons' first house in Parracombe and it was probably at this time that the affair began.

Valerie's husband, Dave Crompton made plans to move to Cyprus. There were long and involved legal problems over the site that he had bought to build a house on. The legal squabbles went on for six years during which time Valerie returned to Devon. She decided, when the problems were at last resolved, that she did not want to go back to Cyprus. She moved to Chelfham.

Mrs Harris admitted later that she had known about the affair from the beginning. Her friendship with Valerie Crompton had ended, and she tolerated Clifford spending nights with Valerie. Some neighbours, in fact, saw Clifford and Valerie as a couple, and knew nothing about their respective spouses. In addition to having to put up with his infidelity, Margaret had another source of discontent. Harris had spent all the money she had brought to the marriage. Police found that he had also spent all Valerie Crompton's money, as well as £10,000 entrusted to him by her mother to invest in a pension fund. The investigation also discovered that Harris was in the habit of spending nights with another lady at a motel, less than 30 miles from Valerie's house.

Their conviction that Harris was responsible for Valerie Crompton's death was reinforced by a number of bizarre phone calls he was making from Australia to friends in the South Molton area, almost from the day of his arrival. 'Are those roadworks finished on the A361?' 'How did Plymouth get on this weekend?' 'Have those new people moved in yet?' It was as if he was initiating conversations in the hope that there would be something important that those he called would want to tell him.

Then there was a hitch in the process intended to bring Harris back to England to face questions about Valerie's death. The Director of Public Prosecutions rejected the findings of the local Crown Prosecution Service solicitors, and said that there was insufficient evidence to apply for an extradition warrant. If police wanted to apply for Harris's extradition they would have also to apply for a local warrant to arrest him for murder; an extradition warrant could not be granted just to enable police to question someone.

When the Devon and Cornwall police told their Australian colleagues about the decision but asked them to maintain their surveillance in the hopes that more evidence would become available, there was some justified resentment. The Australian surveillance had now been in operation for over a week, and they were being asked to continue it indefinitely. Surveillances are expensive to maintain. At least eight officers are required while a subject is moving about, and those officers have to be changed frequently to guard against the subject recognising any one of them as a person he had seen the previous day in a different place. Could that expense be justified? After all, the death that had prompted the operation was nothing to do with Australia. And there was now a further difficulty. The Australian press had picked up the reports in English papers, and the evening TV bulletins were already broadcasting the story about the search for the English couple who had come to Australia leaving a dead body behind them.

It was probable that Harris saw one of these broadcasts. One evening, he left his hotel about 9 pm, walked to a pier in Perth, and placed his wallet, car keys, and cash from his pockets on the roof of a car. He then, still under police observation, walked back into the town to the Royal Perth Yacht Club and disappeared into the deep undergrowth at the side of the river, where he was lost to the view of the following officers. Now they had a double dilemma. These preliminary actions of Harris seemed to be a clear indication that he intended to commit suicide, but if he was followed and had some other reason for this strange behaviour, it would become obvious that he was being watched by police, and, without a warrant, they were powerless to arrest him. The decision was taken to go into the undergrowth, find him, and if it was possible, continue the observation.

When they found him, he was dead. He was lying face down in the river, but he had not drowned. Clifford Harris had choked himself to death by fastening a cord round his neck, tightening it with a stick, and then pushing his hands into the waistband of his trousers so that he would be unable to release the cord.

Margaret Harris, who had been asleep when Clifford left the hotel, woke up two hours later to a TV broadcast that named her and her husband. She immediately called police to the hotel to tell them that Clifford was missing.

That seemed to be the end of the investigation, but there were two other matters to be sorted out. As Harris had died while under surveillance, his was listed as a 'death in police custody' and as such had to be the subject of a full inquiry under Australian law. That inquiry could not be completed until the inquest into the death of Valerie Crompton was held to determine the cause of her death.

Now, although I have told you all the relevant facts, the surveillance on, and death of, Clifford Harris were not my concern when I came to hold the inquest. It attracted international attention because of the suicide of her presumed killer, but the Criminal Law Act of 1977 prohibits a Coroner from naming at an inquest any person known to be, or suspected of being the cause of the death of the subject of the inquest. The verdict was that Valerie Crompton was killed unlawfully, but made little reference to Clifford Harris or his character, and there the matter rested.

4

Suicide Notes

Some suicide notes are spattered with the blood of the writer, quite a few are accompanied by page after page of sentimental poetry. Some victims use the suicide note as a way of causing as much unhappiness as possible to those left behind, one or two are business-like documents, winding up the victim's affairs in an orderly manner. Very few are hysterical or incoherent.

Of the hundreds of suicide notes that I have read, the letter that stays constantly in my mind was a simple, dignified, logical request from a 97 year old lady asking me for the one favour which I was unable to grant. She addressed her letter to the Coroner:

'Dear Sir,
I am writing this to say that I am in my right mind and know what I am doing. My belief is that anyone over 90 years of age has a right to end their life if they really wish to do so. I have had five or more years of happiness at this old people's home, keeping my independence by doing all my own chores. It is a pleasant and kindly home, but I have not been out since last December. I am now weary and full of aches and pains. I don't want to lay in bed or sit in a chair just waiting to die. I really cannot see any sense in living helpless in old age.

I do not wish to live any longer. I am afraid that I might have a stroke and then become a nuisance to other people. My knees do not work properly now, my arteries are worn out. I have cramp-like pains from my feet to my waist and my skin irritates from my toes to the top of my head.

So I am going to end it all as the doctors can no longer help me. None of the sleeping pills I have taken come from this home. I have had them for years.

I ask only one thing. Please do not call this "suicide". Grant my wish and put down, "She just wanted to die".'

Unfortunately the law does not allow me to declare 'She just wanted to die' so I had to record a verdict of suicide.

Perhaps the most damaging note, left with almost vicious forethought, was written by one of the husbands in a case of two young married couples who had known each other for four or five years. Rob and Anne had met Graham and Barbara when each couple had moved out of London to live in the same small Devon village. On this particular Sunday, they had planned to drive to the coast, have lunch at a restaurant, and return in the evening. They lived only a few doors apart. Just before 10 o'clock on the Sunday morning, Rob and Anne went round to Graham and Barbara's house. Barbara was filling a flask in the kitchen.

'Graham's in the garage messing about with the car,' she told them. 'Go and tell him to get ready, Rob, or we'll never get away.'

Rob went to the garage. Graham was dead, hanging from a cross-beam, the chair from which he had jumped lying at his feet. There was a note, clearly written before he went to the garage, saying: 'You three have never really had time for me. I've never fitted into your lives. See how you can get on without me.'

Graham's suicide was wholly unexpected, he had never given any indication of being jealous of the other three, but he effectively ruined their lives. Barbara almost immediately had a nervous breakdown, Rob went into a deep and lasting depression which eventually resulted in Anne divorcing him, and Anne moved away from a house, a job and a village which had all been sources of great contentment to her.

Suicide notes such as Graham's can never be relied on to present a true picture of the circumstances which led the writer to take his, or her, own life. Even suicide notes accompanied by other letters or writings never tell the whole truth. Michael had been separated from his wife and two teenage children for five months. A host of letters and poetry written during those months gave the impression of a heart-broken man abandoned by the only woman he loved.

'You mean more than life itself,' he wrote, more than once, to his wife. At one stage he took a drugs overdose in front of his children after imploring them to ask their mother to return to him. Discharged from hospital, he continued with his barrage of notes and very poorly written poems. He eventually gassed himself in his own car in the garage of his sister's house.

His wife had nothing to say about their separation, nothing to say about the ten-page poems which Michael had pushed through her door, posted to her, or handed to others to pass on to her. A work colleague produced a rambling tape recording that Michael had made two weeks before his death, a recording in which he spoke of his great love for his wife. In a final letter to his mother, he wrote, 'I was betrayed and lied to so much.' His letters, his poems, his appeals to his children, presented the picture of a broken hearted man, deserted by the woman he loved. But the real story was somewhat different.

With all deaths of this kind, we ask for a report from the deceased's GP, or from any hospital he had recently attended. Michael had been referred to a psychiatrist by his GP because 'of his inability to accept the consequences to his family of his numerous and open infidelities'. It says much for the character of his wife and children that they never referred to these 'infidelities'.

The note with which I and my officer, Keith, had the most trouble was one addressed to two people on different sides of the same piece of paper. The dead man had run into money troubles and died through 'carbon monoxide poisoning', the usual inquest description of the results of putting a hose into the exhaust pipe of a car, putting the other end of the hose into the car itself, and closing all the windows and switching on the engine.

The note, left in the car, had been written on a sheet of crumpled paper. On one side he apologised to his 'beloved' wife and assured her that she was not to blame. On the other side, he wrote an almost identical note to his mistress, about whom, we soon found out, the wife knew nothing. As the evidence of the pipe in the car, and the knowledge of his financial difficulties was sufficient to record a suicide verdict, we did not need to produce the suicide note at the inquest. Just in case either lady got to know about it and wanted the note, Keith spent some time straightening out the creases in the paper and making a photocopy of each side.

One of the most vitriolic notes was written by a father to his son accusing his wife of continuous infidelity, and of setting the son against him. The truth, as far as we could tell, was that the man was a cold, unloving bully with no time for his wife or his son and daughter, and who arranged his will before his death to ensure that his wife was left penniless. On the day of his death, he had lunch with his family, played, for the first time, a computer game with his son, and then walked out of the house and shot himself in a nearby field.

To anyone present in his court, a Coroner may appear to know very little about the person who is the subject of the inquest. The facts given are meagre, the victim is identified, the cause of death is established, only rarely is it necessary to carry out a lengthy investigation into the cause of death. Any accounts given by witnesses, families, friends – and sometimes enemies – may be coloured by the way an individual wants the deceased to be remembered. In a drugs overdose, the parents may claim that their son or daughter had fallen into bad company. In cases in which insurance payments may be disputed, the deceased's earning potential may be exaggerated. In only a handful of cases, do people lie deliberately, and then it is usually a matter of a mother wanting to withhold something shameful about a child, children concealing that they hadn't visited a lonely parent, workmates pretending that a colleague was not a drunken risk taker.

But Paul's case was different. Paul spoke for himself. He had a passion for making video films. To be honest, his passion was not matched by any skill. He knew how a camcorder worked, but he had little idea of the niceties of handling the instrument. Framing the shot, editing, even making certain that the dialogue could be heard by the viewer, seemed to be completely beyond him. He just pointed the camcorder at his subject and switched on. He filmed his family watching television, he filmed neighbours walking along the street, he filmed himself working on DIY jobs around the house. I was a little surprised to find that he even owned a camcorder. Working in a dead end job for £120 a week, and supporting his girlfriend and their child, how could he afford such comparatively expensive equipment?

The last video he ever made had all the faults of his other efforts, indistinct dialogue, the camera set at an awkward angle, and complete failure to take account of changing light. But he had tried some editing, and whether it was deliberate or accidental, it added immensely to the poignancy of the film itself.

The video begins with Paul, his girlfriend Sarah, and their daughter Sylvia aged 18 months, sitting in front of a television in their living room. The television itself is playing while Paul films Sarah getting Sylvia ready for bed. Neither Sarah nor Sylvia take any notice of the camera, so we can assume that filming was a regular event. We also know from other film, that it was quite common for Paul to use the camcorder while the television was playing.

Paul's voice on the sound track, Sarah's obvious happiness, and Sylvia's ease with her mother and father indicate a very secure and happy family group. Next there is a short shot of Paul mending the roof of a garden shed, and then we are in Paul's car, with the camera on the passenger seat and Paul talking directly to it. He has difficulty fixing it so that his face is fully in shot, but he finally succeeds. He is on Dartmoor on a fine summer's evening, the sky is clear. He smokes while he talks.

'Feeling pretty shitty to tell the truth. Just making this test to see if the camera is working.' The film then switches to another shot of his daughter playing in the garden, before coming back to Paul. He lights another cigarette and begins talking to the camera again. In a very matter of fact way, free from any trace of self pity Paul is filming his last hours on earth. The video is his suicide note.

Two weeks before, he and Sarah (they had lived together for four years) had decided to marry. Sarah was overjoyed at the decision. Her parents had never been comfortable about her live-in relationship with Paul, and were equally pleased. Paul had not been nagged into proposing. As he said at the time, 'It's the right thing to do for Sylvia.'

As part of her preparation for their new life, Sarah had

decided to spring clean their flat, and to throw away all those things that had been stored away in cupboards and boxes, because 'they might come in handy one day'. In the top of a wardrobe in which Paul kept his one suit, she found a video. She pushed it into the recorder while she carried on with other work in the living room. Perhaps it was a blank that Paul had forgotten he'd had, or one of the many videos he had made of her and Sarah, starting with the day she had brought the baby home from hospital.

Yes, it was a family video. The first shots were of Sylvia when she was about 18 months old. Sarah went on with her cleaning, listening rather than watching. Then with her back to the television, she heard a man's voice, a voice she did not recognise, and turning round she saw the video was showing a homosexual act. She stopped the video in terror, and composing herself, replayed that section hoping that some impossible technical error had superimposed Paul's face onto a pornographic movie, or that Paul had been given the video because the man looked so like him. But there was no error. She saw the mark on Paul's right shoulder that she knew so well. There was a distinctive sweater lying on the floor that she had given Paul last Christmas. She did not recognise either his partner, or the room in which this nightmare was taking place, and in less than a minute the video had moved back again to her own flat, back to what up to then had been a normal and happy life.

That evening, Paul tried to explain that his quickly admitted bisexuality did not mean that he loved Sarah and Sylvia any the less. Sarah was alternately cold and hysterical. Paul had to leave. There would be no marriage. She would have to think about whether or not she would let Sylvia see him. They could sort out the details later, but he must go. He would have to go on supporting her and

Sylvia. She made it clear that, like many others, she thought that homosexuality was the same as paedophilia, and that their daughter was in danger of being abused.

Paul left the flat that evening, and slept in his car. Significantly, he took his camcorder with him. He spoke to Sarah on the phone in the morning. She was sorry for him, but there was no way she would have him back. We don't know what he did during the day – he didn't go to work – but he was now in his car on a bright summer evening on the edge of Dartmoor preparing to kill himself. He talks half to the camera, half to himself, lighting one cigarette after another. Sometimes he rushes what he is saying so that it is difficult to hear him. Sometimes he speaks slowly and deliberately; there are many long pauses. There is no indication that he is drunk or has taken drugs. His tone is as detached as that of a man discussing the progress of a football team he does not support.

'Pretty quiet here... Haven't really done anything wrong. Being bisexual I suppose was lying to Sarah... Hoped we could have a relationship without me doing the other. Just hasn't worked out like that. Not really worth it. No one will understand it.'

He switches the camera off, and when the film resumes he is lighting another cigarette. The sky behind him is a little darker, and behind Paul's head there's a tree as still as death. During the next four hours he uses the camera as a letter to Sarah and to Sylvia, as a report on how he's feeling, and even as a commentary on what is happening on that particular part of Dartmoor. It becomes clear as the video progresses that although he is determined to die, he is also looking for excuses to delay his suicide.

'It's five past nine. Soon as it gets dark, I'll put the pipe in the back and gas myself. Least that's the plan. Made sure there's enough petrol in the tank. Going to lock all the doors. Can't be seen from the road... Seems to be some sort of track here... Just do it and get it over with. Everything I have goes to Sarah, doesn't need saying. Just wish it could have worked out different.' Then another long pause.

'Thing about dying is you're on your own.' At the cinema or on television such a phrase would come across as cheap sentiment. When Paul says it, it's the genuine realisation of a simple and honest man. Then the camera is switched off. Was this the point at which he intended to gas himself?

But the film begins again. This time Paul appears to have rehearsed what he wants to say next.

'Just say a last few goodbyes to everyone. I got no alternative way out really. The camera and the car goes back to Sarah. That goes without question.' Then there's another long pause, as if he is having second thoughts about what he intended to say. 'It's getting darker, about twenty five to ten now. It's quiet here. This is where I'll be staying. Think I'm nervous? Morelike I'm petrified.' He pulls a sweater on over his T shirt, and lights another cigarette.

'Hope whoever finds me doesn't have a heart attack. Two bodies at the same time won't look good... Still don't know what to say. I didn't mean to upset anyone. It's a good night to die. Sky's lovely. Lovely clouds. Soon be up there. Won't be floating though, morelike hanging down.' Paul, who has been looking up at the sky, now turns back to face the camera.

'Send you all my love anyway, especially to Mum. Been a crappy life. Never knew what I wanted from one moment to the next. Just hope I can get on with it. Don't feel so upset now.' The camera is turned off again. When the film resumes, Paul is lighting another cigarette.

'This is a message for my little girl. Your mother will probably respect me for what I'm about to do. She wants me to get out which is understandable but she wants me to support her. I get £120 a week. There's no way I can do that... You're a cracker of a baby. If it hadn't been for my stupidity, things would have been different. But I can't keep lying and cheating. Just can't keep it going. I do love you. [Paul is now clearly talking to Sarah rather than his daughter.] Know it sounds crazy. What happened just happened; it doesn't take any of my love away from you or Sylvia.'

The film stops. When it resumes, it is darker outside, and the car radio is playing. It's now ten o'clock. Paul apologises to everyone again, including the police who will have to deal with him. After a pause he says, 'Something inside tells me that I won't go through with this.' The film stops. When it restarts again, Paul is in a detached, objective mood.

'Lot of kids shouting and screaming somewhere. I'm all alone apart from the radio. Even the sheep seem to have disappeared.' His face is now in profile against a blue evening sky, with the smoke from his cigarette drifting across the screen.

'Getting really dark now. Ain't afraid of the dark. There's nothing in the dark that ain't there in the daytime.' Then, almost as an aside, 'Can't afford to live on my own and keep Sarah and the baby,' and brusquely, 'Going to sign off now. Give all my love to everyone. Sorry again.'

He puts his cigarette out. 'Okay, this is it.' And then, perhaps the most disturbing sequence in the whole video, he stands, or half crouches, looking towards the camera and in an unnaturally loud and facetious pseudo-American accent shouts, 'Goodbye and see you all on the other side.'

But that wasn't the end. About an hour later he starts filming again.

'It's five to eleven. Punters racing around here in cars. Couple of young lovers parked down from me, so I'll have to wait until they go. Give it an hour. Have a few more fags. Pollute my lungs. Not that it matters... Just hope the hosepipe works.'

He reports back at midnight. 'Just plug the holes up and start the car. I'll keep the video running. Hope this is quick.' The next sound (the screen is now dark, although the film is still running) is of Paul assembling the hosepipe leading into the car from the exhaust. Incredibly, he is humming to himself as he works. Then the camera angle shifts, and shows the lights of a town a mile away, and a few seconds later car headlights at the edge of the town. The cars are speeding round in circles, with the drivers executing hand brake turns.

'Bloody boy racers. Police want to do something about them,' Paul says. At this point someone must have approached Paul's car or have been near it, perhaps a wife looking for an errant husband out on the moor with his mistress. Whatever happened, it is clear from the next extract that it was enough to cause Paul to move to another site. Presumably he had to dismantle the hosepipe from the exhaust, and reconnect it when he stopped.

'Half twelve now. I'm in a quiet field. Like Piccadilly Circus that other place. Sign off now. Let's see what happens.' The film ends, as Paul had arranged it, with a shot of him working on the garden shed, and Sylvia playing in the foreground.

Twelve hours before he died, Paul had spoken on the phone to Sarah who told him, 'You're the best thing that ever happened to me.' At one stage, during the four hours he was preparing to die, Paul asked in real bewilderment, 'Why did you never tell me that before?'

He need not have worried about having enough petrol in his car. The engine was still running when he was found twelve hours later by a farmer in whose field he had committed suicide. He said Paul was 'very grey and stiff' and the hosepipe that he had worried about was still securely in place held by masking tape to the exhaust. All the doors of the car were locked. The farmer called police from his house, and on their advice returned to the car with a neighbour, broke one of the windows with a rock, unlocked and opened all the doors and disconnected the hose.

The inquest lasted for not more than 20 minutes. Keith, my Coroner's Officer, read out the formal statements from the farmer who found Paul and from the constable who reported the death. I returned a verdict of suicide.

There was no need for me to make public one significant fact. It would only have added to the grief of his friends and family, and was of importance only to Sarah, who emigrated shortly after the inquest. Three years earlier, Paul had sought medical advice for his impotence. The GP had recommended some minor surgery, but Paul had decided not to go ahead. His notes show that 'his partner knew of the condition and was very supportive.' So, it follows from the birth of Sylvia, that Sarah had found an answer to Paul's impotency. This can have only added to her anger when she found that Paul was using what in fact was her gift to him, to be unfaithful to her with another man. My verdict simply recorded that he took his own life following an argument with his wife. There was only the routine reference to the 'suicide note' at the inquest.

5

A Nice Place to Die

There are very few occasions on which it is necessary to have a jury at an inquest; one of them is when the death has occurred while the subject was in prison or in police custody. It is clearly in the public interest that any death in detention should be investigated thoroughly. If there is the slightest suspicion that someone has acted wrongly by using too much force, or by neglecting obvious safeguards, then the Director of Public Prosecutions decides if there is sufficient evidence to found a criminal charge. When there is no such suspicion, a Coroner must hear all the relevant evidence so that the public, and the relatives of the deceased, can be satisfied that the death was unavoidable.

On an August evening in 1991, 31 year old Ronald Andrew Steffano, who had a string of convictions for violence, theft, and possession of drugs, was driving a Honda Civic through Torrington in North Devon. PC Jim Bailey, the driver of a local police car, had been given the number of Steffano's car as one which had been 'behaving suspiciously' a few minutes earlier near an isolated house outside the town. The caller had told the police control room that he had seen the Honda parked in a lay-by, with the driver walking up and down, apparently looking at his house. PC Bailey had seen the Honda travelling towards Torrington, and had pulled behind it with his blue light illuminated and his headlights flashing. He knew nothing then about Steffano, but just wanted to question the driver of the Honda about his reasons for stopping in the lay-by.

Steffano accelerated immediately, reaching speeds of 65 mph in Torrington's narrow streets. At one point he drove over a grass verge to travel in the opposite direction. He passed a roundabout on the wrong side, and forced a number of on-coming cars to swerve out of his way. PC Bailey stayed behind him waiting for the seemingly inevitable crash. At the bottom of a hill Steffano attempted to overtake a lorry by driving onto the pavement and passing it on the inside. This time, he misjudged the gap and the Honda hit the front of the lorry. Steffano jumped out, ran across the road and climbed over a low wall. PC Bailey, after telling his control room what was happening, followed him.

He saw Steffano go down another embankment and begin to climb down towards the edge of the Torridge. At this point he was only 15 yards away from Steffano, and shouted to him.

'Look. It's very steep down there. You'll break your neck. Come back up here.'

Steffano stayed where he was, and the PC, caught in the undergrowth and hanging on to the branch of a tree, continued to urge him to give himself up. Both men were out of breath, and PC Bailey was wisely playing for time, knowing that other officers were on their way to help him. Suddenly, Steffano dropped further down into thick bracken, and again disappeared from view. The officer realised that the only way for Steffano to escape him was to cross the river which was about waist deep at that point.

Steffano did, in fact, cross the river, and was seen by the wife of a farmer on the river bank who asked him what was wrong.

'I've crashed my car,' Steffano told her, 'all through that pig chasing me.' He put his finger to his lips to warn her to keep quiet, and ran across the farm into a small stream at the other side of the field. The farmer's wife then saw PC Bailey and another officer who had joined him, and called out to them, indicating where Steffano was. The two officers traced him to a footbridge under which he was hiding and arrested him. At that stage, of course, other than his reckless driving, they had no evidence that Steffano had committed any offence, but common sense made it clear that someone who was at such pains to escape police must have something to hide.

Taken to Barnstaple Police Station, Steffano at first refused to give his name. His clothes from the waist down were soaking wet, and he was given a green boiler suit to wear while his clothes dried. When he did provide his name, the police computer gave particulars of his previous convictions, and details of an offence for which he was currently wanted, grievous bodily harm on his pregnant wife from whom he was separated. Police computer records carry warnings of particular types of behaviour – 'violent', 'suicidal', 'drug user', 'always alleges assault by police' – so that custody officers can be aware of potential problems. Steffano's record was marked 'Violent. Drug User.'

During the course of a long tape recorded interview, in the presence of a duty solicitor (the lawyer who attends a police station to advise a prisoner who has not got his or her own solicitor), Steffano refused to answer questions coherently, claiming that tape recordings made when he had been charged with other offences had been cut about to make him 'sound like a ———– idiot'. When he was asked what he did for a living he said that he 'read tarot cards and the stars'.

He was shown a piece of cannabis that had been found in his car. When it was placed on the table in front of him, he picked it up and ate it, and then denied that it had ever existed. At one point he said he had been looking for a cliff to drive his car over. He described the assault on his wife as 'giving her a few digs'. Grievous bodily harm is more than 'a few digs'. His wife had been beaten so badly that she had to be admitted to hospital.

The interview had lasted for just over 30 minutes. The officers conducting it commented that while Steffano had appeared vague and rambling, whenever straightforward questions were put to him that might incriminate him, he avoided answering them. They therefore saw his remark about driving over a cliff as part of a strategy to make them believe that he was not responsible for his actions.

Steffano was returned to his cell. The cell block at Barnstaple was almost full, but the gaolers still had time to provide Steffano with another change of clothes. The boiler suit which he had been given on his arrival was also damp, and he was provided with a track suit from a bag of clothes found in his car. As the major charge against him was the GBH at Southampton (he had actually attended the Crown Court but had run away before his case was called) he was kept at Barnstaple until an escort from Hampshire could collect him.

During the rest of the morning and the afternoon he was seen by various police officers who described him as quiet and coherent, and at 2.30 pm, two lay visitors (volunteers who are allowed to attend police stations unannounced at any time during a 24 hour period to check on the treatment of prisoners) spoke to him, finding him co-operative and coherent, if slightly withdrawn. At 5.30 pm, Steffano hanged himself in his cell.

As it was August, and very warm, all the cell hatches had been left open; the hatches are one foot square doors set in each cell door so that meals can be passed to anyone detained in the cell without opening the door itself. Steffano had reached through the open hatch of his cell door and tied the legs of his boiler suit to the door handle, and had then tied the arms of the boiler suit around his own neck before slumping to the floor and strangling himself. You may be surprised that a man can hang himself without jumping from a chair or ladder, but door handle suicides are not uncommon; the mere act of dropping to the ground with a noose around the neck can be as effective a method of strangulation as the more conventional kicking away of a support to leave the body dangling.

As soon as he was found, police began resuscitation attempts which were continued by the ambulance crew and a doctor. Steffano was still breathing when he arrived at the hospital but was already brain dead. His life support system was switched off six hours after his admission.

The death of anyone held in custody, be it in a police cell or in a prison, is a proper matter of concern. Periodically, MPs voice that concern, sometimes on behalf of an individual constituent, sometimes to raise their own political profile. One of the first MPs to raise the issue did not know that there was a full inquest into the death of anyone who died in custody, nor is it generally realised that 'in custody' covers people on their way to a police station, or on their way to or from hospital, and hospital patients who have been arrested prior to their admission. Nor do the minority of people who view any inquest into such a death that does not accuse the police or prison authorities of crimes ranging from murder to callous indifference as an establishment whitewash, appreciate just how thorough the subsequent investigation can be.

In Steffano's case, we have already seen that he was interviewed in the presence of an independent solicitor who he could have asked to see at any other time. He was also seen by independent lay visitors whose only purpose is to ensure that prisoners are being treated properly, and to take note of any complaints they may make. Some large police stations now have the cell passages and custody suites monitored by 24 hour video cameras. All prisoners in police cells have an individual custody record showing at what times they are visited, fed, released from their cells, or visited by police officers. When a prisoner dies, the subsequent inquiry is conducted on the lines of a murder investigation with the cell being sealed, all relevant property taken by the investigating officer, who interviews everyone who has seen the prisoner since the time of his arrest, and anyone who can provide further information.

Steffano's mother, who had been notified of his arrest, before his suicide, was also interviewed. She said that her son had been depressed for a long time, and had once, after coming out of prison, told her that he would rather 'top' himself than be locked up again. Unfortunately, she did not pass this on to the police officer who told her of Steffano's last arrest. The two ambulancemen, and the doctors and hospital staff who had dealt with Steffano were also interviewed, as were all the police officers, including gaolers, and the farmer's wife who had seen him come out of the river.

All this evidence was presented at the inquest, and I was satisfied that there had been no way in which the officers who had care of Steffano could have anticipated that he would have committed suicide, despite his statement in the course of the rambling interview: 'I was just touring round looking for a nice place to die.'

6

Come In Woolly Mammoth

An Open verdict at an inquest means that the evidence available is not sufficient to determine the exact circumstances of death; it may have been a suicide, it may have been accidental, in some very rare cases, it may even have been an unlawful killing. The witnesses may have their own opinions, the Coroner can only base his verdict on the facts.

There were over a dozen people involved – Dr Snuggles, Garfield, Scarecrow, Double Diamond, Starlight, Tiger Lady, Kinky Devil, Rockhopper, Kissogram, Denver, Gemini Lady, Soundman, Spangle, and Woolly Mammoth himself were all CB (Citizen Band Radio) users in South Devon. They cruised the villages, towns, and hills on the edges of Dartmoor in their secondhand cars talking to each other, sometimes across a couple of streets, sometimes from hill to hill, sometimes from one side of Dartmoor to the other. The CBs were their 'rigs', their nicknames – self selected – were their 'handles', and their meetings were 'eyeballs'.

South Devon is ideal country for CB users. The hilltops afford clearer reception and transmission – 'we could pick up signals from as far as Wales,' said one of the group. The isolation of the countryside also allows the use of small amplifiers – 'burners' – to increase the CB signal, but which, if used too near a built up area, interfere with domestic radio and television. Woolly Mammoth had a burner, and was very careful about its use. Fifteen years ago, as a teenage CB user, he had been banned from the air waves by his fellow enthusiasts because he was constantly interrupting other transmissions. Fifteen years ago also, he had a different nickname.

Jim Tanner, to give Woolly Mammoth his 'straight' name, was born in 1965 in Tavistock, and at the age of three contracted a rare disease that left him covered in bruises. His father said that he looked as if he had been badly beaten. He was cured, the disease never returned, and he was never seriously ill again. He was a non-smoker, a moderate drinker, fit, well over six feet in height, and liked by everyone he met. Well, nearly everyone. When he left school, he went to work for a company making paving slabs. He was then living in Torpoint, and became the butt of his companions' jokes. They called him 'Chicken George' because he looked after the poultry at a local school, and progressed to bullying Jim, rather than just having jokes at his expense. No one ever found out why he was bullied. Jim, described by a friend as being 'sensitive, someone who walks away from an argument, easily hurt by anyone who called him names', would never discuss it, other than saying it was his problem, he would sort it out.

In 1988, Jim started work in Sussex, coming home at weekends. He was then 24, and met a 15 year old girl. The girl's parents clearly didn't object to the relationship. She and her parents came to Torpoint one Christmas and stayed with Jim and his family, with the girl, then over 16, sleeping with him. In 1992, Jim had to leave the family home. He had refused to take one of his aunts shopping, and the family decided he would have to get out. There was probably more to it than that. He regularly took members of his family to the shops, being the only one with a car, and had even arranged insurance so that one of his friends could do the shopping trip if he was working. He had to sleep in his car for two or three months. There was no way that his girlfriend could contact him, and the relationship ended.

If the breakdown in the relationship affected him, he gave no sign of it. His friend, Starlight, said that he always kept his feelings to himself, apart from one occasion when he found him in tears. He was then living back in Torpoint, where he had been teased earlier in his life.

'Those rumours have begun again. People know I'm back here again. I feel like doing something stupid like driving into a wall or over a cliff.' When Starlight tried to cheer him up, he wouldn't explain what the rumours were about. He recovered quickly and 'seemed to be normal again'.

As far as Starlight knew, Jim had no real problems. Although he was always short of money, he paid for private dental treatment, subscribed to the AA, and took out life insurance. He always paid in cash, and never used a cheque book or a credit card. After the girl from Sussex, he had no regular relationships. Starlight knew of a couple of 'one night stands' which seemed to owe more to the lady's initiative than Jim's. Another CB user described him in a rather old fashioned phrase as being 'fond of the ladies'. He did seem to have an unusual liking for very young girls, often calling out to 13 and 14 year olds as he passed them in his car, embarrassing Starlight, who would recline the passenger seat and attempt to sink out of sight. The only trouble he had ever been in with the police concerned his driving documents, and he was once arrested because his car had been seen near the scene of a robbery, but nothing further came of that.

Two or three nights a week, Jim became Woolly Mammoth staying out until 4 am, talking to other CB users. There was never anything significant about these conversations – 'Big crowd in Union Street tonight... I'm going to buy some crisps... Kinky Devil and Spangle were around last night' – but there was a clear satisfaction in being able to talk to friends and strangers on a virtually private network. Conversations might result in 'eyeballs', which were rarely more than a cup of tea and biscuits at one user's house. There was, however, a great deal of mutual support. A CB user who wanted to borrow a roof rack, pick up a spare tyre, get a lift into Plymouth, who had run out of petrol – a fairly frequent request – had only to ask on the channel, to be sure of an offer of help if anyone was near enough.

Once, Kinky Devil and Spangle (there were as many female as male CB users) were being harassed by a stranger in a mini on Dartmoor. Their call for help was answered by Woolly Mammoth whose arrival frightened off the man in the mini. The only thing Jim had to be frightened of at that time was another group of CB users who sold rigs. Jim also sold secondhand rigs, well below their prices, and claimed that he had been threatened by one of them.

At the beginning of November 1992, Gemini Lady was riding with Woolly Mammoth when thick smoke started coming from the dashboard of his car. She called for help on the CB and Desert Fox turned up with Mario. Jim said he would wait for the AA to come and sort the problem out, and the other three left him there. Later, Jim fixed the problem which had been caused by faulty wiring of the CB rig, by running a wire directly to the battery, rather than to the cigar lighter point which was its normal power source.

The next evening, 2nd November, Woolly Mammoth had an eyeball with Double Diamond who was able to recall, in astonishing detail, that he had a coffee, two custard creams, a mini Mars bar, and a mini Aero.

Just before midnight that day, a number of CBers heard Woolly Mammoth calling for Denver, who was believed to be a girl living in Ivybridge. Earlier in the evening he had been the victim of a practical joke when Dr Snuggles, a woman CB user, had contacted him, pretending to be another female CBer, and invited him to meet her at a pub in Plymouth. She contacted him by radio when he arrived at the pub, and told him of the joke, which Jim took in good part.

Around midnight, Woolly Mammoth was near the top of Brent Tor, a few miles from Kit Hill from which he had been broadcasting. He told a man called Checkpoint that police had asked him to keep an eye out for anyone setting fire to cars in that area. He also told other CB users that there was a man in a Capri who kept passing him and looking at him. 'I'm OK. I've got a big hammer in the back of the car.' That was the last time anyone spoke to Woolly Mammoth. No one heard him sign off, a CBer's indication that they would not be speaking again that evening.

About nine the next morning, Woolly Mammoth's car was found near the top of Brent Tor, completely burnt out. It was recognisable only by the index plate. The news was quickly circulated round the CB community. A forensic report said the car had been destroyed by a 'moderate' explosion probably caused by a bare wire igniting petrol fumes. The area within a radius of 30 feet around the car was covered in debris from the explosion. Very soon CBers learned that there was a body in the car. But whose was it?

The corpse was unidentifiable. The hands and forearms, the feet and lower legs, and the front of the body had been completely burnt away. There were some teeth left in the upper jaw, but the face and top of the skull had also been burnt away. The body had been considerably shortened by the fire so there was no way of knowing the original height or weight. It could not be identified from fingerprints or from dental records. The presumption must be that it was Jim. He had been heard broadcasting from the area around midnight. The only other link to connect Jim to the car was a surveillance video film taken at a local garage around 7 pm. It showed him filling his car with petrol, filling a petrol can, and driving off. It seemed fair to assume that Jim was in the car when it caught fire.

But how did it catch fire? The police examined the possibility of murder. During his last transmissions, Jim had said that there was 'A man in a Capri who seemed interested in me. I'm not worried, I've got a big hammer here.' Was the man in the Capri one of the CB dealers who objected to him selling cut rate rigs? The police found very little evidence that there was such a group of dealers, and there was nothing to indicate that Jim had been killed before the fire. They ruled out foul play. That left the inquest with a choice of accidental death or suicide.

Why should Woolly Mammoth have committed suicide? He had this undefined problem with 'the rumours'. He had been separated from a girlfriend who clearly meant a lot to him, a year earlier. In the evening before he died, he complained of a stomach problem. He'd just been cheated out of his rent money by a friend who had arranged new lodgings for him.

None of his friends, however, detected any signs of depression in the days before his death. One CBer who talked to Jim shortly before he died, described him as 'distant and quiet, but in good spirits'. Many people who have already planned their suicide are in surprisingly good spirits, they have made up their minds and have come to a decision which will end their problems. So being cheerful is no indication that a person had not already decided to kill him or her self. And, in Jim's case, there was the incident of the whiskey.

Jim's body was found in a burnt out car at Brent Tor, one of the favourite sites in Devon for CB users.

On 2nd November, Jim met Starlight and gave him two bottles of whiskey as Christmas presents for Starlight's mother and sister. This might be the typical behaviour of many would-be suicides who want to put their affairs in order before dying, or it could just be that Jim, who was having problems in finding somewhere else to live, wanted to escape the inconvenience of carrying the bottles around with him.

If the fire was caused by a bare wire accidentally igniting petrol fumes, why did Jim, who was electrically competent enough to rewire his rig after the first fire in the dashboard, allow such a danger to exist? He had bought a spare can of petrol that evening, and, according to friends, he always carried such a can in the footwell or in the boot.

Was it then an accident? A fortnight before, Jim had told two fellow CBers that he was thinking of torching his car to claim £400 insurance money. There was also the strange conversation on the evening of his death about police asking him to look out for people setting fire to cars. Was this an inept cover for his own intended burning out of his own car?

No one will ever know just what happened after midnight on Brent Tor. The inquest recorded an Open verdict.

7

It's A Man's Life

A Coroner sometimes has to hold an inquest on a person who has died abroad, even when another inquest or inquiry has already been held in the country in which the death occurred. This happens when the body is returned to England for burial or cremation, and thus comes into the ambit of our laws which require an inquest to be held on any dead body within the Coroner's jurisdiction. Here are two examples of the process at work.

It was what Ray had joined the army for, a foreign posting. Nineteen years old in Blackburn with only dead end jobs in view, the posters in the recruiting centre were as attractive as those in the travel agents. 'Let The Army Make a Man Of You', something like that, with the implication that in the process the army would be taking you to countries where the sun shone all the time, where off duty hours were spent touring sites that civilians had paid hundreds of pounds to visit, and where work involved armoured vehicles, computers, high powered weaponry, and the company of like-minded young men.

Of course, it hadn't been quite like that, but he was enjoying it. He was fitter than he had ever been, the NCOs and officers were the best bosses he had ever had, not like the flat-nosed bawling martinets that most movies had led him to expect, and much more intelligent than the two or three foremen he had worked under as a labourer. And he was abroad. When he heard he was going to Brunei, he anticipated the long golden beaches and blue seas of the tourist and army posters. Well, this was not exactly a golden beach. Perhaps they'd go there at the weekend. Just now they were in the jungle, a fairly damp, gloomy jungle, being trained in jungle warfare. It was sticky, tiring, stressful, even a bit dangerous, but, all in all, a damn sight better than digging holes in the road, or stacking pallets with a low loader. Ray Jones was glad that he had joined.

Tuesday, they spent attacking a village. The village had been built by the Royal Engineers, a handful of huts, and a sort of square in the centre. No one had ever lived there. It had been built just for this sort of training. The village was empty, and they were using live ammunition under the very close supervision of the NCOs. One of the sergeants had explained that some of the objectives of the exercise were to get them used to moving through unknown country firing live rounds; to get them used to the noise; to train them to pick concealed positions from which to fire; and, most importantly, to habitually check that their line of fire did not cover any of their fellow soldiers who might have worked their way ahead of them. This wasn't a full exercise when you'd be under fire yourself, just an initial training exercise.

After it was over for the day, Ray, and his three mates, Tigger, Ken, and Baldy, stood round a table cleaning their rifles and sorting out the live ammunition that was left. One of the NCOs collected it all, and then issued them with blanks for use on the following day. They filled their own magazines with blanks – each man marking his own magazine with a strip of insulating tape to ensure that he would pick up the right one after they had finished cleaning their weapons – and then filled a spare magazine with another 30 blanks. They also each fitted a Blank Firing Attachment to their rifle, a device which breaks into tiny fragments anything that comes out of the barrel.

Wednesday's exercise was going to be different. Some of the NCOs and the admin staff would be in black overalls representing the enemy. This time the 'enemy' would be in the village not returning fire, just being there to give the platoon something to aim at. The 'enemy' would take cover, but would be watching the flash from the muzzles of the approaching guns. If they thought they'd been hit, they would fall to the ground. The instructions were to 'double tap' anyone you thought you had killed once you got near the body; that is you fired two shots into the head to ensure that the 'enemy' was dead, and not waiting for you to pass before shooting you in the back. The double taps in this exercise were to be fired to one side of the 'dead' opponent.

Wednesday morning around seven, they started the attack. Ray, like the others, had his full magazine of 30 blank rounds loaded the previous night, and the spare in his rucksack. It was up to them whether they fired in bursts or in single shots, but as one of the instructors pointed out:

'You won't know how many people you are up against. You won't know how long you'll be fighting. You won't know where your next supplies are coming from. You do know that you're all marksmen capable of killing with one shot, and that we'll be expecting you to double tap every kill.'

So they started off about a mile from the village. They had to approach without being heard and without losing touch with each other. Ray felt tense but confident. He and his mates moved quickly and efficiently. Ray kept his eye on Tigger who was following the Corporal, and made certain that he could be seen by Baldy who was behind him. To his right and left he was aware of the other two sections following the same routine. They soon disappeared into jungle, and Ray's section pushed on to the edge of the village.

They paused. The drill was to find good cover from which you could shoot, once there was something to shoot at. There was nothing moving in the village, just houses to watch. Ray waited. Then a black overalled figure came from a house on his left about 50 metres away. He took careful aim and fired one shot, and was immediately startled by the fusillade of shots from all round him. As he loosed off a short burst, he remembered the Corporal's warning the previous evening.

'Thing they'll do is this. Soon as they reckon you're in position, they'll get just one man to walk across. Real easy target. So we've all been waiting, getting just a bit edgy, and everyone opens up. Enemy know straight away how many of us there are, and whereabouts we are as well. So, for —— sake, don't shoot the first man you see. Wait until there's plenty on view and go for the target who's directly in front of you.'

Ray looked at the Corporal. With his left hand he signalled everyone to stay still. Now that their cover was gone, it was down to the platoon sergeant to decide on the next move. He might choose to retreat and try again around sunset. Eight hours sitting tight in the jungle would teach them to hold their fire next time. He might opt to stay put, and see what the enemy reaction was. It looked as if he'd gone for the second. They were staying put. Meanwhile, the 'enemy' who had been well and truly shot lay still on the ground.

While they were waiting, Ray had a funny thought. No one had ever indicated whether the 'enemy' were civilians or soldiers. Would he really be expected one day to open fire on a village full of civilians? What about those places in Vietnam? The Yanks had no way of knowing if they were about to enter a peaceful village, or one where the villagers were Vietcong who would open fire on them as soon as they thought they were safe. Another thing, his

BFA was missing. He must not have fixed it on properly. Should he let the Corporal know? Probably wouldn't matter. They were only firing blanks at a distance so no one would be within range of any fragments. Be a bit dodgy when it came to the double-tap though. Still, cross that bridge when we come to it.

Then, people began to appear from the houses. Several of them walked slowly towards the 'dead' man, and bent over the body. No one fired. It hadn't been an order, it was almost instinct. There would be more. Wait until there were more targets. Instinct was right. The 'enemy' had assumed that the mistake on the opening shots had caused the platoon to withdraw. More of the 'enemy' came into the open square. Directly in front of Ray, perhaps 50 metres away, was a bench, and two of the enemy, Sergeants Williams and Evans sat together on it. Williams was a smashing sergeant, knew the job backwards, always willing to help and advise. If you weren't going to make it, he had the guts to tell you so, and to suggest alternatives. A proper manager.

Well, now he was the enemy, and the Corporal lifted his hand. Ray fired at Sergeant Williams, or rather to his left side. Even though they were using blanks, the standing instructions were to shoot to the side of the intended target. The flash from his rifle must have been obvious to the Sergeant who clearly acknowledged that he had been killed by slumping backwards on the bench. Sergeant Evans ran for the cover of a house but another burst of fire 'killed' him, and he fell to the ground. Ray fired at two or three other 'enemies' and then the Corporal signalled for them to advance into the village.

They were still on the edge when a whistle blew signalling the end of the exercise. This sometimes happened when one of the observers had decided that there had been a major error, or that the exercise was at a point where an immediate advice and training session would have more impact than a debriefing later on. Ray looked for the platoon sergeant with whom they would all rendezvous, and saw the 'dead' Sergeant Evans stand up and call to Sergeant Williams who was still slumped over the back of the bench. So laid back, that Williams, he had probably taken the chance to grab forty winks.

'Come on, Williams boy,' shouted Evans. 'No need to be dead anymore. Work to be done.' But Williams did not move. Evans ran to him, and took him by the shoulders, and then pulled the front of his overall away. There was a small wound over Williams' heart, and just the slightest trace of blood round the wound.

'He's dead!' shouted Evans. 'He's dead! He's been shot!'

At the subsequent army inquiry – the Brunei government had agreed that the death could be handled under British jurisdiction – and at the inquest when Sergeant Williams' body was brought home, it was established that every weapon that had been used in the exercise, and all the spare magazines, had been collected, within 15 minutes of the death becoming known. In addition, every soldier was searched by an NCO from another platoon to ensure no one was carrying any live ammunition. From the outset, Ray Jones had been identified as the person who had shot at Sergeant Williams. Sergeant Evans had located the bush from which he had seen the flash, and had also confirmed that both he and Sergeant Williams had seen the barrel of Jones' rifle just before firing began, and had noticed that there was no BFA attached.

The post-mortem on the unfortunate sergeant showed that he had been killed by a small section of a live round which had pierced his heart. Jones himself had little doubt that the bullet had come from his gun. Williams had slumped back immediately after he had fired at him; his fellow soldiers had all been able to identify their own targets. From the moment he realised that Williams was dead, he had felt sick with fear. The NCO who checked his magazine found that he had fired four blanks, then a live round, and then another three blanks. Jones knew nothing of how the live round had become mixed in with the blanks.

'Did you check the blank rounds as you reloaded?' asked the examining officer.

'Yes, Sir. We were given a box of blank ammunition, and we loaded from that.'

'Can you tell the difference between a blank and a live round?'

'Yes, Sir.' It was later established that the two different rounds of this particular type of ammunition were almost identical. Live ammunition was never counted, so there was no way of checking the source of the fatal round. Even if Jones had been careless and had left one live round in his magazine from the previous day, there was no way it could have worked its way up the magazine to become the fifth round to be fired.

No one would have dropped the live round into the box of blanks deliberately; that would have been to risk himself being the victim. It must have been left there accidentally. The only verdict could be Accidental Death.

Another inquest that I held into a body brought back from abroad also involved a shooting, but was the only inquest in which I've been involved that included evidence of a lie-detector test, or, as this was a death in America and we should use the correct American term, a polygraph test.

Annie Jones had married an American serviceman and was living with him on a military base in Albuquerque, New Mexico. Annie had been married before, and her former husband had won custody of the only child of the marriage, a daughter. It would be natural for an American court to award custody to one of its own citizens, and there is no reason to believe that the decision was in any way critical of Annie.

On the day of her death, she had been out shopping with her husband, and on their return, after unpacking the shopping, had helped with some carpentry in his workshop. In the evening, before settling down to watch television, Annie asked her husband to look at the trigger action of her Magnum revolver. She had quickly taken up the custom of her fellow wives on the base and had armed herself for her personal protection on those occasions when her husband would be away from home.

Darren, her husband, told the military investigators that he had taken the Magnum out of their gun cabinet in which he kept 'all their guns', made certain it was unloaded, and noticed that there was one live round loose in the bottom of the holster. He examined the trigger with Annie, and they each 'dryfired' the gun a number of times while ensuring that the trigger was working correctly. Annie had often fired live rounds in the woods around their home, so she was quite used to the action of the gun. After a while, Darren left Annie to go to the bathroom. On the way back, he heard a bang, and saw that Annie had shot herself in the side of the head. When he reached her, her heart was still beating, but she had died before he could phone for help.

As a normal part of their investigation, the military police asked Darren to undergo a polygraph examination during the course of which the following questions were put to Darren, to all of which he answered 'No'.
- Did you see your wife place a bullet in the gun?
- Did you place a bullet in the gun?
- Do you know anything about what happened prior to the weapon being fired?

• Are you withholding specific information about your wife being shot?

When the results were analysed, Darren was told that the machine indicated that he had been lying. He then told a different story.

He and Annie had been indulging in some horseplay with the gun, in the course of which she must have put a live round in the chamber. He was certain that it was not him that had put the bullet in the gun. Had he loaded it, he told the examiner, he would have used the full six rounds. He emphasised that they were not playing Russian Roulette, nor did either of them ever point the gun at the other. The other relevant point that he had omitted in his previous statement was that Annie had drunk a jug of wine, about a litre, and over half a bottle of whiskey. She had shot herself in the right temple when he had been out of the room. This time the polygraph indicated that he had told the truth.

Although there was some evidence that Annie had been depressed over the separation from her daughter, there was no indication that she intended to take her own life. The verdict was therefore, Accidental Death.

8

The Door Is Always Open

I hope you do not get tired of my constantly emphasising that a Coroner has no responsibility for apportioning blame. The death of Shirley Webb, at first sight, seemed eminently preventable, but could anyone really have saved her from herself?

The new beat bobby for the village was going around introducing himself to everyone: shopkeepers, single mums, the old and the lonely, the young and hopeful, the kids at the village school. Stan Davis wanted to know them all, and wanted all of them to know his face. No one had been able to tell him much about the bungalow on the corner.

'Never seen them, to tell you the truth. Keep themselves to themselves. Never see them in the shop. Think there's two of them, but I'm not sure.'

The garden gate was off its hinges, The path had disappeared under tangled weeds and undergrowth. If there ever had been a lawn or flower beds they were now similarly buried. Stan wondered if he had been directed to a derelict house. Most of the windows had been broken, years rather than weeks ago, and had been repaired with pieces of hardboard or the backs of cardboard boxes, held in place by sellotape. The front door was partially open. He pushed it and called, 'Anyone in?'

He didn't expect an answer. The hall was completely bare, no covering on the floor, wallpaper so dirty that it was difficult to tell if it had ever borne a pattern, a wire hanging from the ceiling with no bulb or shade. But there was someone there. A voice from a room on his left asked him to come in.

His first thought was that his colleagues at his new station had staged a very elaborate joke. There was very little light in the room because of the broken windows. There were theatrical swags of cobwebs hanging from the ceiling and in every corner of the room, webs made rope-thick with years of dust. The only pieces of furniture he could see were an armchair and a settee.

In the armchair sat an old man in filthy clothes, his face unwashed and unshaven. On the sofa lay a woman, just as old, just as unkempt, just as filthy. In a surprisingly strong and educated voice, the woman asked what they could do to help the officer. Lost for words, he stumbled through his routine speech about being new to the area, wanting to know everyone, and could he do anything for them. The old man answered, again, in a firm and educated voice.

'That's very kind of you officer, but no, we're perfectly all right.'

What about the broken windows? Were they having trouble with vandals?

'No. Not any more. The children used to break them when we were out at work. We were both teachers. We're retired now, of course. They don't bother us anymore. Must be six years since the last one was broken.'

Bewildered, and at a complete loss, Stan took his leave.

'Don't close the door,' said the old lady as he left. 'We can't get it open if it's closed.' Stan was about to offer to fix it, but there was something about their self assurance that convinced him that they would refuse to let him do it.

Back at his police house, he phoned the local social services. Yes, they knew the couple very well, Brian and

Shirley Webb, brother and sister, aged 66 and 64 respectively. Refused every offer of help made to them. The council was about to apply for an order to force them to have their septic tank cleared, as it was becoming a health hazard, but there was nothing else that could be done. They had both had recent falls which had resulted in a brief period of hospitalisation before they were allowed home, and the hospital staff had reported that they were poorly nourished, but otherwise healthy, and regular visits from a district nurse confirmed that there were no grounds on which they could forcibly be taken away.

Senior staff had been to the bungalow, unwilling to accept that their juniors had done everything that could be done, and had come away as bewildered as Stan had. One of them, looking around while his colleague spoke to the Webbs, had found £5,000 in bank notes which he persuaded them to put into a building society, opening a new account for them.

Then, the curse of the British winter, a burst pipe, came to the help of Stan and the social services. There was a sudden hard bitter frost. The Webbs' bungalow was flooded by a burst pipe, and a surprised fire crew called out by neighbours to deal with the flooding, shocked at the conditions in which the Webbs were living, called for Stan, who immediately called out the social services. The Webbs could now be put into an old people's home while the bungalow was repaired. The council took advantage of the Webbs' absence to mend the pipes, clean and redecorate every room, fix the front door, and empty the septic tank. They also installed gas fires, as the bungalow had no other heating.

The Webbs returned to their sparkling new home. Stan came round to see them. They were sitting as they were when he first saw them. The social services had already told him that they had refused an offer of new furniture. Yes, they had quite recovered from the shock of being flooded out. No, there was nothing that they wanted. And 'don't close the front door, we can't open it.'

This time, the council ignored the wishes of the Webbs and allocated a home help to them who called at the house four times a week. They allowed her to do the shopping, but would not let her clean anything. She bought them, at their request, packets of crisps, fruit pies, Kit-Kats, and pasties. They ate nothing else. Sometimes, she told the social services, she had seen them eat pasties with mould growing on the top which they had covered in tomato sauce. They smoked a lot, and each week gave her £20 to bank in their name. Occasionally they gave her sums of £100 to put in their building society account. The money must have been sent to them through the post.

They never had visitors. They never washed or changed their clothes. They never used the bedrooms, sleeping in the chair and on the settee on which they spent their days. They never used the gas fires. When she complained of the cold, they would allow her to turn on one bar of the fire. She discovered that, as soon as she had left the house, they turned the fire off again. When the social services directed that they be given meals on wheels, in spite of their many refusals to accept the service, the home help noticed that Shirley never ate the meals provided, usually giving hers to Brian.

Within two years of the redecoration the bungalow was beginning to look as dirty and neglected as ever. Stan still made regular visits and kept in touch with the home help, but had accepted that the Webbs were a couple beyond help.

Then, Shirley Webb, having not been outside her bungalow for over two years, was seen at 1 o'clock in the morning sitting, fully clothed, on the pavement outside the house. A youth, who had once been one of her brother's pupils, saw her and asked if she was all right.

'I couldn't make out what she was saying,' he told police later. 'I'd heard that there was something funny about her, so I thought she was drunk, so I left her alone.'

A little later, a young man and his girl friend walking home, saw Shirley sitting in the middle of the road. They did not speak to her. 'Didn't know who she was,' they said later. 'Anyway, she looked a bit funny, a bit frightening.'

Half an hour later when the same young man came down the road on his motor cycle, Shirley was still sitting in the middle of the road. 'She swayed as I went past,' he told police, 'so I knew she wasn't dead. I didn't speak to her as I didn't know what to do.'

About seven hours later, a neighbour, who lived across the road from the Webbs, found Shirley's body on his front door step. She had clearly died of exposure and malnutrition. Brian, clearly now unable to be left on his own, was moved into an old people's home. Afterwards Stan spoke to the home help.

'What was this thing about always leaving the door open?' he asked. 'They kept saying that if it was closed, they couldn't open it.'

'That's right, they couldn't,' she told him. 'They both had had accidents and had broken bones. Everywhere she went, she sort of shuffled round on her bum, and he couldn't walk properly either, so he crawled everywhere on his hands and knees. Neither of them could reach the door handles, so they left all the doors open and they wouldn't get locked in.'

So Shirley Webb spent her last hours on earth and the last vestiges of her strength shuffling across the road, at one in the morning, to contact a neighbour to whom she had never spoken. No one will ever know why.

9

Whatever Happened To So-and-So?

We'll never know just how many suicides leave themselves a little loophole, a little opportunity for someone else to intervene before that very last moment.

How many times have you been watching a television programme, and been prompted to ask yourself, 'I wonder what happened to that fellow who used to be a presenter on this programme?' It could be a comedian who used to have his own series, of whom nothing is now heard. It could be a documentary reporter famous for exposés, when did you last see her on screen? Remember that chap in Brookside? Has he been in anything since? Television must be the hardest job for anyone to leave. One year you're recognised everywhere you go. You're asked to speak at dinners, open fetes, take part in chat shows, then your TV career finishes, and twelve months later someone else is in favour. The wise ones know what's coming and make provision for the day. Others hope that something will turn up.

John was one of those who hoped that something would turn up. He had been a popular evening presenter on Scottish TV. His contract had finished, his wife had left him and gone to Canada. There were no offers, or even hints of more TV work in Scotland. He lost most of his money in a business that failed with his partner declaring himself bankrupt, leaving John to face the debts. His only asset was a flat rented out to an unemployed waiter. So he came to Devon to settle and to look for work. There was no work, and he only had enough money to rent a room in a friend's house.

For a year he stuck it out in what he described as 'a rain-swept Devon town with no friends, and the prospect of asking people for loans.' Although he was an agnostic he joined the local Church of England choir. His landlady paid for his telephone calls, loaned him small sums of money, and even paid the interest on his mortgage for the flat in Scotland. The local doctor attempted to help him with his unhappiness over losing his job, and the vicar welcomed him to the church, albeit as a singer rather than a worshipper. But John was going nowhere. He could see no future, and at the beginning of April, he began planning his suicide.

He drew up a will, asking his solicitor to accept it as a legal document, 'as I haven't the time or money to go consulting expensive legal specialists and getting it absolutely accurate.'

The real object of the will was to ensure that all those to whom he owed money were paid. His flat in Scotland was to be sold, and the proceeds used to pay off his overdraft, the outstanding mortgage, his solicitor, and money owed to his landlady. The residue was to be divided between two friends, one of whom was the husband of his half sister living in New Mexico, 'who took me in when I was orphaned and gave me the opportunity and education to pursue my life with a set of kindly principles and a trained mind.'

John also had a set of woodworking and other tools, and perhaps his real character can be judged by his instructions for their disposal.

'All the tools for woodworking and maintenance in my

South Molton church where the victim sang in the choir.

work shop are to go to the young instrument maker in the garages adjacent to the parking lot in South Molton. His courage in starting a difficult business on the slimmest of budgets has impressed me, and I want these to go to someone who will use them with discretion and skill.'

Finally, he scrawled a note to his landlady apologising for being rude to two of her friends ('my mind was understandably on other things').

Then he drank a bottle of cheap wine, sat down on a chair in the entrance hall ('It will be less messy there') and putting a shotgun under his chin, literally blew out his brains.

Ironically, when the shotgun came to be sold as part of his estate, it was found to be in such poor condition that it had only scrap value.

We always ask a victim's doctor for any comments he or she might have about a patient's condition, and John's doctor very discerningly described him as 'not depressed but frustrated.'

There was only one question mark about John's suicide, a question that can never be answered. He wrote a number of letters indicating his intentions, dating them from April 14th onwards. These were all left with his will to be found after his death. But he wrote a short note to the vicar asking him to intercede with God for the sin of taking his own life, and posted it, by first class post on the day before his death. That letter would have arrived anytime between 8 and 9 am on the 28th, the day John died.

John's last note indicated that it was 8.30 when he had finished the bottle of wine, without specifying if it was am or pm. It is more than likely that John shot himself in the evening, but what if he had been up all night? His suicide letter did say he had taken sleeping tablets and that they hadn't worked, 'so I'll have to use the shotgun', which might indicate that he had taken the tablets and hoped to die in his sleep. In which case it would have been 8.30 am when he decided to shoot himself, and there was a possibility that the vicar would have already received his letter and would have come immediately to his house.

When the vicar did read the letter, that's exactly what he did, but, as he had been away for a fortnight, he did not read it until five in the evening. And the post-mortem revealed that there was only a small amount of drug from the sleeping tablets in John's stomach. Had John really hoped that the vicar would call before it was too late ?

10

The Front Seat Passenger

This was one of the rare cases in which I had to consult with the Home Office about holding an inquest on the death of a woman whose body could not be found.

On 21st December 1996, Polly Levon called in at her local butcher's in Silverton to buy sausages. Silverton, a village north of Exeter, is the sort of place in which everyone knows everyone, where there are few visitors, a friendly place. No, she told the lady who served her, the sausages weren't for the Christmas dinner. With Derek's new business doing well, they could afford something better than sausages. These sausages were going abroad. She and her husband were taking the sausages to Cyprus. They were going to spend Christmas with their two daughters on that island, and the one thing they had been asked to bring with them was a couple of pounds of Silverton's famous sausages.

The Levons had often been to Cyprus; indeed, they had lived there for a short time. Polly was looking forward to the trip and especially, to seeing her six grandchildren. There was the usual exchange of 'Merry Christmas' and, 'if I don't see you before, a very happy New Year', and Polly Levon went out of the butcher's, full of the joys of the season. To all those who knew her in Silverton, and to her daughters to whom she spoke by phone every week, Polly was a very brave woman. It was common knowledge that she had been suffering from cancer for four years, but she had never appeared to let it get her down, nor did she ever complain. She'd had an operation, and there was nothing further that could be done. Let's get on with life.

She chatted to another friend in the road outside the butcher's. She'd changed her lottery numbers that week, and, of course, the original numbers had come up. Still, no use worrying about that. She was off to Cyprus to see her daughters and grandchildren. It was going to be a wonderful Christmas.

That was the last known time that anyone saw Polly Levon alive. Neither she, nor her husband, went to Cyprus. Polly had packed her suitcases, told her daughters the time they would be arriving, and arranged for a neighbour to keep an eye on their house, but Derek, her husband, had never booked the tickets for the flight.

At 5.15 pm, that day, a friend called at their house to deliver a parcel. Derek told her that Polly had suddenly had to go to London as her mother had been taken ill. Later that day he told one of their daughters that the Cyprus trip had been cancelled as Polly had food poisoning.

Two days after Christmas – the only time that Derek had been seen over the holiday was late on Boxing Day when a neighbour saw him in front of his house – there was a fire at the Silverton house at six in the morning. The fire brigade arrived quickly enough to stop it spreading, and acted quickly enough to discover that the fire had been deliberately started. In fire brigade parlance there was evidence of an 'accelerant' on both floors of the house, two metal cans which had probably contained petrol.

The chief officer passed his suspicions on to the police who were already on the scene; it is standard practice for police to attend the scene of a house fire where their responsibilities may range from diverting traffic to tracing keyholders for unoccupied premises. A quick check showed that there were two people listed as living at that address; there was no sign of either of them. As soon as it was possible, police and fire officers searched the burned out building.

There were no signs of any bodies, and the chief fire officer's professional opinion was that the fire itself had not been of such an intensity that the bodies of any persons who had died in the house would have been reduced to ashes. Indeed, two fully packed suitcases were found, almost undamaged, in a bedroom. Neighbours, with the exception of the man who had seen Derek on Boxing Day, were unable to provide any useful information, other than that on the two nights before Christmas, all the lights on the upper floor of the house had been on all evening.

Police then circulated their own and neighbouring areas with a message giving details of the fire and indicating that they wished to speak to the owners of the property, Derek Levon aged 61 years, and Pauline – known as Polly – Levon aged 59 years. The message also gave the registration numbers of the Land Rover and Volkswagen cars owned by the couple. The Land Rover was still at the house, but the blue Volkswagen Passat was missing. There was a very quick response from Tiverton Police Station. The Levons owned a 100 acre property near Witheridge known as West Yeo Moor Farm. One of the buildings on the farm was a large barn. Officers were being sent immediately to see if the Levons were there.

At that stage, of course, police realised there were a number of possibilities. The Levons could be working at the barn, oblivious of the fire that someone else had started at their home. They could have started the fire themselves to claim the insurance money, and gone to the barn to establish an alibi; fires started for such a purpose are often discovered and extinguished long before the fire raisers intended. The Levons could have gone to Cyprus; checks were being made at Bristol, Exeter, Gatwick and Heathrow airports. Those were the obvious alternatives. But there was another factor which became known while police were searching the records to find out what else was known about the Levons. Derek was the owner of five shotguns, each properly recorded on his certificate.

Police going to the farm were told of the possibility of Derek being armed, and warned that if there was the slightest suspicion that the Levons were there, to take no action until armed colleagues had arrived. Almost at the same time, another search of the house at Silverton found a metal gun cabinet with three shotguns still in place. Derek had either taken two guns with him, or had two guns at the farm.

A police helicopter flew over West Yeo Moor Farm but could see no sign of the blue Passat in the open, though it could be hidden in the barn. At 1.30 pm, police found Derek at the farm. He was sitting in his Volkswagen, with a sawn-off shotgun pointing to his head and a pipe leading into the car from the exhaust. The car was visibly full of exhaust fumes, and Derek was obviously in the process of killing himself by carbon monoxide poisoning. The farm was quickly surrounded by police and all roads leading to it blocked off. Trained negotiators attended with a contingent of armed officers.

Most police forces now have negotiators, specifically trained to understand and to converse with people who may be temporarily unbalanced, about to commit suicide, and/or armed. The police philosophy is that armed officers should only shoot as a last resort if the subject is about to kill another person or a police officer. The police preference is to persuade the subject to put aside whatever weapon he or she may be using, and they are prepared to talk for hours to achieve that objective. Devon and

Cornwall officers were particularly concerned that there should be no precipitate action; at that time there was still an outstanding complaint against some of their colleagues involved in the shooting of a Devon farmer who had been threatening his neighbours with a shotgun which he had fired on a number of occasions.

Constable Colin Mitchell, the negotiator dealing with Derek Levon, was only able to conduct a rather one sided conversation with him. One of his objectives was to open some sort of dialogue with Derek in the hope that he could be distracted from his suicide bid. Derek had turned off the car engine, but remained with his shotgun pointing at his head. Never once did he turn to look full face at Colin or at the other police. On the few occasions he replied to Colin, he opened the car window but kept the muzzle of the shotgun against his face with the stock supported against the steering wheel and his finger on the trigger.

At one stage he told police, 'It doesn't matter what you say. You won't change my mind.'

Later on, to the question, 'Do you know where your wife is?' he answered, 'She's with me in the car', and held up a small metal box.

When he was asked if police could speak to his wife, he told them that he had written a note to Tiverton Police Station on Boxing Day 'that would explain everything'. (When the letter was subsequently found at the station it said that he and his wife had 'decided to leave this life together. She has preceded me. Polly's out of it now. She didn't suffer.' Derek had signed the letter which was dated 26th December 1996.)

At another stage during the attempted negotiation, Derek asked Colin for his name. Later, he was seen sobbing, and, just before 3 pm he opened the window to tell Colin, 'I'll do it at three.'

At 3.01 pm he put the shotgun into his mouth, and

pulled the trigger. The police at the scene were so shocked that they were immediately taken off duty, and other officers were brought in to deal with the search of the farm. Their first concern was to find Polly, who, Derek had claimed, was in the car with him.

Well, her ashes were in the car. On the passenger seat beside Derek's body was a long metal tin that had originally contained a bottle of Glenmorangie. On the lid of the tin was a label saying: 'This is my wife. Bury her with me.' Inside the tin were a quantity of black ashes, some pieces of bone, and a small piece of metal. The message on the lid was repeated on another label inside the tin.

There had obviously been a fire outside the barn. There was an area of burnt grass, a circle of concrete blocks around the charred area, wood ash in the middle of the blocks, and two or three corrugated metal sheets which had been burned on one side, and which, on the other side, had a covering of black ash.

Inside the barn, police found a spent shotgun cartridge, and straw covered in dried blood. There was a presumption that Polly Levon had been shot in the barn, or had shot herself, and that her body had been subsequently burned to ashes. In the discussions following these finds, one officer who had spent some time in Cyprus suggested that the Levons would have been familiar with the common rural practice in that country of building a kiln out of doors by putting up a rough circular stone wall, lighting a wood fire in the centre and covering the fire with corrugated metal sheets. The heat generated is enough to cook meat on, or even to completely burn unwanted animal carcasses or other rubbish.

But was it Mrs Levon who had been burned? The ashes from the box, together with the bone and metal and the ash from the top of the corrugated sheets, were submitted

The barn in which Derek Levon talked to police for over an hour before shooting himself.

to the Forensic Science Service. Their findings were that the ashes in the box and the ashes on the corrugated sheets were from the same adult body. The piece of metal had come from a woman's bra, and the bone had come from a skull. The FSS had examined the bone very closely and had found a mark on it and were satisfied that the bone bore traces of lead. It was possible to take DNA samples from the blood in the straw, from Derek Levon's body, and from their two daughters who had come over from Cyprus. Scientists were able to say that it was a 490,000 to one chance against the blood and ashes not being those of Mrs Levon.

The police were finally satisfied that Mrs Levon had been shot in the barn and that her body had then been burned in Cypriot fashion by her husband. The letter sent to Tiverton Police Station on Boxing Day indicated that she was already dead, but there was nothing to show whether she had shot herself, with, or without Derek's agreement, that Derek had shot her in a suicide pact, or that he had simply murdered her. There were two other questions. What had happened to the missing shotgun? Derek had five, only four of which had been found. If Mrs Levon's body had been cut up, where had it been cut up, and what had been used? The questions were answered, or partially answered, five months later. The farm at Witheridge had been put up for sale by the executors, and a potential buyer visiting the property found that a small pond which had been frozen over at the time of the police search had dried up in the abnormally rain-free spring. Now, at the bottom, it was found to contain a meat cleaver, and the dismantled pieces of a shotgun.

My first problem, as a Coroner, was to obtain Home Office permission to hold an inquest on Polly Levon. There was much circumstantial evidence that she had indeed been killed, that she had died in my Coroner's district, and that the body on which I wanted to hold an inquest had been reduced to ashes. There was no absolute proof at this stage, without forensic evidence, that any of these assumptions were true. Fortunately, the Home Office accepted my submission and I was free to hold the inquest.

Prior to that inquest, there was a lengthy and detailed police investigation which, with the assistance of the Forensic Science Service, and the pathologist, had to establish conclusively that Polly Levon was dead, and how, when, and where, she died.

The pathologist who assisted me, fortunately, had great experience of cremation procedures in this country, and of funeral pyres in India and Pakistan. His opinion was that, for a body to be completely reduced to ashes, the funeral pyre would have to burn for 12 to 24 hours. To

Derek had used corrugated iron sheets to burn his wife's body.

reduce a body to ashes in a shorter time, it would have to be cut into small pieces. In this respect, the evidence of a neighbour living next door to West Yeo Moor Farm became very important. On 21st December, at about 1 pm, he had seen Derek Levon at the farm. Derek was unusually nervous, and had locked the farm gate behind him, which was equally unusual. Around 3 pm, the same neighbour had seen a large fire about 100 yards from the barn; we know that Derek was back in Silverton at 5.15 pm.

The police inquiry also found that Polly Levon was not suffering from cancer. Her GP had no record and the hospitals at which she told friends she had received treatment for the condition had no records of any such treatment, and the scars which she had shown her daughters, claiming that they were the results of an operation for cancer, appear to have been those left by an hysterectomy.

There was also an extensive inquiry into Derek's business affairs. His associate, Gordon Pirie, told police that their fortunes had changed in 1990 when their very successful electronics business, based in Surrey, had begun to fail because the Ministry of Defence had reduced its requirements. In 1995 the company was bankrupt, and a second company, into which Derek had put over £100,000 of his own money, failed at the end of 1996. At a staff Christmas lunch on 19th December, Derek was asked what he was buying Polly for Christmas, and had said that he had already decided what she was going to get. Later, it was found that he had cleared everything from his office on the day that the lunch was held.

On 24th December, when Gordon rang Derek to wish him a happy Christmas, Derek said that Polly was in hospital. He also told Gordon, 'It's been a pleasure knowing you', a remark which puzzled Gordon at the time, and which only became significant with the news of Derek's death.

The inquest into the death of Derek Levon was comparatively straightforward. There was no doubt that the man sitting in the car at West Yeo Moor Farm was Derek Levon, and that he killed himself. As far as Polly Levon was concerned, there were a number of other factors to be considered.

She had been seen alive on 21st December. Later that day, Derek Levon had told a neighbour that Polly had gone to London to her mother's. At 8 pm, he phoned one of his daughters to say that Polly had food poisoning and would not be coming to Cyprus. On 24th December he had told Gordon Pirie that Polly was ill.

On 21st December, three hours after Polly had last been seen alive, Derek was at West Yeo Moor farm in a state of some agitation. At 3 pm there was a large outdoor fire burning on the farm. Ashes recovered from the farm, and blood found on straw at the farm were linked by DNA to Polly. An empty shotgun cartridge, found in the barn, had been fired from one barrel of the shotgun with which Derek had killed himself. My finding, therefore, was that Pauline Levon had been unlawfully killed.

11

Twins

Most deaths have an obvious cause, most suicides an understandable reason, but, now and again, there is no explanation for the way in which a life is suddenly ended.

They had started their lives together, and now it seemed they would finish their lives together. Jean and Jenny were twin sisters. They had been to the same schools, had the same friends, worked in the same library until they were in their twenties when Jenny married a childhood friend. Jean approved of the marriage, she liked Stephen; it wasn't one of those triangles in which one sister steals the other sister's man. They had been good friends as well as sisters, and Jean was genuinely sorry when Stephen, promoted in his job, had to move away from the town in which they had all grown up.

The sisters stayed in touch. Jean never married, but was godmother to Jenny's first and only child, Bernard. Stephen died of cancer when Jenny was 70, and Jean was on hand to comfort her. She had long retired from her post of librarian, and lived on her own. It was logical for the sisters to move in with each other. Jean had only a one bedroomed flat, Jenny a two bedroomed house. Bernard, now aged 40, still lived at home, so where would Jean sleep?

'We always slept together when we were little girls. We could go back to doing that.' It worked. Later, both confessed that they had their doubts about the arrangement. It was true they were still very good friends, but sleeping together after all that time?

'We've all got funny little habits that might irritate other people. We get used to doing things our own way. It can be bad enough in the kitchen, but worse in the bedroom,' they told one of their mutual friends. 'But we manage very well. It suits us.'

There was a period when Jenny seemed very depressed. Everyone put it down to her husband's comparatively sudden death. Jean was full of life, and just the sort of companion that Jenny needed. But the same friends who noticed the sister's contrasting moods, began to notice a change. Jenny slowly recovered from her depression and became the cheerful outgoing person she was before Stephen's death. Now it was Jean who was depressed. The doctor didn't understand her, wouldn't give her the right pills. She wasn't sure that she had done the right thing moving in with Jenny. After a few weeks, her mood changed again. She apologised for things she had said when she was depressed.

'Don't know what was wrong. Anyway, that's in the past. Hope it doesn't happen again.'

On this particular morning, Jenny was up at 7.30 am as usual making breakfast for Bernard, and seeing him off to work. Just after 8 am she went back to the bedroom. Jean had not yet got out of bed.

'Do me a favour, dear,' Jean asked Jenny. 'Close the window. It's much colder than I thought.'

Jenny walked over to the large sash window which had been opened to its full extent and was about to pull it down when she heard Jean behind her.

'I'll get you, I'll get you,' Jean was screaming, and before Jenny could turn round, she felt two belts thrown round her throat and pulled tight.

She struggled round to face Jean who, face contorted,

was pulling the belts tighter and tighter. As she put her hands up to try to loosen the belts, Jean hit her in the mouth, knocking her false teeth loose, and then with her right hand pulling hard on the belts, pushed her left hand into Jenny's mouth, pulling and tearing, and clearly attempting to get her fingers down Jenny's throat.

Jenny, almost unconscious, fell to the floor. Jean continued to pull on the belts and to push her hand deeper into her mouth. Jenny then passed out.

When she came to, she was bleeding heavily from her mouth, and the belts were still pulled tight around her neck, but there was no sign of Jean. She staggered down to the front door and fell again to the ground before she could open the door and call for help.

At the back of the house, a neighbour, Mrs Brown had gone into her garden to put food out for her dog. Looking over towards Jenny's house she was astonished to see Jean hanging by one hand from the window sill of the first floor bedroom. Jean also saw her and called out that she was going to jump. Mrs Brown recognised that there was nothing practical she could do to help or stop Jean, and ran back into her house to dial 999.

It seems incredible that a frail 70 year old woman could hang onto a window sill by one hand, but for however many seconds that Mrs Brown took to get back indoors, get to the phone and dial 999, Jean hung on. It was only when Mrs Brown went as near to the back door as her phone lead would allow her that Jean let go. The fall was less than 20 feet. She sustained massive fractures and died before an ambulance arrived.

A second neighbour who had seen Jenny and who had also telephoned for an ambulance took her into her own house. At this stage she did not know what had happened to Jean, but in the next few minutes, with neighbours, police and ambulance crews arriving almost together, she understood that Jean had thrown herself, or had fallen out of the bedroom window.

'Don't let me go in the same ambulance,' she begged. She went to hospital in a separate ambulance and soon learned what had happened to Jean. She could remember little of what her sister had done to her. She could clearly remember the last thing that her twin had said to her.

'I'll get you. I'll get you.'

12

Helping A Dying Man

The argument for and against euthanasia may be summarised as a plea for allowing those suffering from an incurable and painful illness to be assisted in ending their own lives, and a warning that such a change in the law would permit the irresponsible to rid themselves of unwanted relatives. But that debate does not touch on the dilemma faced by anyone who comes across a suicide in progress, a suicide which could be prevented.

It would be only basic humanity to attempt to dissuade, or physically prevent, someone about to throw him or herself from a high bridge, although it might be argued that anyone who paused long enough to enter into dialogue with a would-be rescuer had not completely decided to commit suicide. In this book, you will read of two cases in which the victims wrote suicide letters well in advance of their death in circumstances which suggested that there might have been an almost unconscious hope that someone would intervene before they died. Dr Jenkins faced a different problem.

Jonathan Mayfield was 84, and had been stone deaf since he was 17. He had been very happily married for 50 or more years. In spite of his disability he had a very happy and fulfilled life, and often described his wife, Jenny, as his ears. Their relatives saw them as a contented and self sufficient couple who never needed, and who certainly never asked for, help.

Then, at the beginning of January, Jenny died. Jonathan was characteristically philosophic about her death. He was happy that she had been relieved of the double burden of her own illness and of looking after him. He had become increasingly arthritic and was confined, for most of the time, to a wheelchair.

He went to Jenny's funeral on crutches, and, according to friends and relatives, was cheerful and positive in his attitude. After her death, his next door neighbour, Gillian, who had been employed as a home help, gave him extra assistance, coming in several times a day to ensure that he wanted for nothing. It became a daily routine for her to wake him every morning around 9 am and to look after his shopping and other domestic chores.

On 21st January, when she went to waken him, she found him sitting up in bed but in a deep sleep. As she was unable to wake him, she left him thinking that perhaps he was unusually tired, but when she returned at midday, he was still asleep and still in the same position, so she called the family doctor.

Dr Jenkins came at around 1.30 pm, noticed Jonathan's heavy breathing and unconsciousness, and also saw two letters, one addressed to him, and one to Gillian. He opened the letter addressed to him which said:

'I have taken 50 Sonyrel tablets and some gin... If there is a spark of life, please let me go. I will go to my Jenny rejoicing.'

The letter to Gillian confirmed his intention to kill himself, and gave the telephone number of the undertaker he wished to arrange his cremation.

Dr Jenkins had a difficult decision to make. He could, as he said later, arrange for Jonathan to be taken to hospital but he did not think that he would live long enough to get there, or he could respect the clear last wishes of his patient. He chose the latter course.

He explained to Gillian what was happening, and told her that he would 'obey the old man's wishes'. Then he left, telling Gillian that he would be back in the evening. When he returned at 9.30 pm, Jonathan's condition had not changed. He intimated that he expected Jonathan to be dead by the morning, and told Gillian to ring him.

She rang at 9 am on 22nd January telling him that Jonathan now appeared dead. Dr Jenkins took a number of other calls, and at 10 am phoned the police, and asked them to meet him at Jonathan's house. When he went to the house, Jonathan was, indeed, dead, and he issued a death certificate. In fairness to Dr Jenkins, he seemed surprised when the police told him that this was a matter for the Coroner and that he could not, as he had intended, issue a cremation certificate. With their permission he phoned Jonathan's daughter and told her exactly what had happened. It is also fair to point out that the daughter supported his action then and subsequently.

There was now a police investigation. Dr Jenkins, on his solicitor's advice, said almost nothing. Gillian told the police what she knew and what had happened. There was some police speculation that she might be prosecuted for aiding and abetting whatever offences the doctor may have committed, but such an idea was soon dropped, and she was seen as the chief prosecution witness, albeit an unwilling one.

A report was submitted to the Director of Public Prosecutions suggesting that Dr Jenkins be charged with manslaughter by negligence, and/or the minor offence of aiding and abetting a suicide contrary to section 2 of the 1961 Suicide Act (the act which decriminalised suicide and attempted suicide). The DPP decided that there was insufficient evidence to prosecute and referred the matter back to the Coroner's Court.

This was an inquest with a jury, and among the evidence

submitted to the jury were statements from three independent medical practitioners indicating that had Jonathan been sent to hospital when Dr Jenkins first attended him, there was a chance that he would have survived, though for how long, and in what state of health, they were unwilling to speculate. I directed the jury that there were only two possible verdicts that they could return.

The first was unlawful killing, which would be the correct decision if they found that Dr Jenkins had been guilty of manslaughter. Manslaughter in this case, I told the jury would cover the absence of any intention to kill, but would encompass an element of unlawlessness in intending to carry out an act, or omitting to carry out an act where there is a duty to act, and thus being grossly negligent as to whether or not death or serious harm would be caused. In reference to such an act or omission it would be necessary to prove that was the cause of death.

The second possible verdict would be that the deceased killed himself.

I also pointed out that there was no obligation in English law to save someone who was in danger of dying.

The jury decided that Jonathan had killed himself.

13

No Comment

It is not a Coroner's function to make comments on the lifestyle of the deceased, or on that of any witnesses who give evidence at an inquest, but I could not have been the only person astounded by the sheer irresponsibility of 29 year old Tom Spring, an irresponsibility that seemed to be shared, to a lesser degree, by some of his friends.

Tom's five year old marriage had ended in separation. His wife left him on more than ten occasions during those five years because of his heavy drinking. She kept returning, he kept promising to cut down his drinking, but nothing changed, and she finally left and started divorce proceedings. During one of her absences, Tom accidentally set fire to the kitchen. It was his habit, when he had come in from an evening's drinking, to cook chips and sausages for himself. The unattended chip pan caught fire, and the kitchen had been destroyed by the time the brigade arrived.

While his wife was away, Tom looked after, or, it might be more correct to say, should have looked after, their two children Lesley aged three, and Amanda aged 18 months.

This particular July day was spent as Tom had spent so many others. Just before noon, he went to his local pub. Being a dutiful father, he took his two children with him. He stayed drinking there with friends until the early evening. It was not unusual, according to one of those friends, for the unemployed Tom to drink 20 pints of strong lager during a day's drinking. No one indicated where the money came from for boozing on that scale, and that afternoon, no one was keeping count.

Around six, Tom decided that the children must be fed and took them back home. None of the friends who gave evidence later on about this day, mentioned the children; it was almost as if they had not been there.

At about 7.30 pm, more friends called at the house to take him out drinking.

'I've done it again,' he told them, almost proudly. He had had another chip pan fire which he had put out himself, but not before the heat had melted a plastic clock on the wall above the stove, and had completely blackened the stove itself.

They all started off. 'What about the kids?'

'They'll be all right. They've had a good day. They'll be asleep in no time.'

But one of the women who had called at the house had a little more compassion. 'I'll stay. You can pick me up when you get back.'

She stayed until just after midnight, and went home, after asking a neighbour to keep an eye on the children. Tom and his friends went from pub to pub. At two in the morning when there was nowhere left to drink, Tom and another man went for a swim in the sea, before Tom returned home, apparently unconcerned that his two children were alone in the house.

The next day began in the same way. Tom and his two daughters went to The Bell in Appledore. Tom had three pints, and left there with his children, and some friends to go to The Anchor, where they had a few more pints. Then another pub, another pint. By six, Tom had already drunk twelve pints. No one is very clear about what he did with the children. He must have taken them home, and given them a meal, but by eight o'clock he was back drinking, with the children again at home, again unattended. He and his friends drove, yes drove, to a string of other pubs, drinking a pint in each. Around midnight, they went into a pub in which one of Tom's brothers was already drinking. By that time Tom had drunk, at least, 17 pints.

'He didn't look drunk,' his brother claimed. 'He was very happy, very sort of relaxed, but not drunk.'

At about 1.30 am, one of Tom's friends dropped him off at his house. A neighbour who saw him before he went indoors said that he looked quite normal. He was quite steady. No sign that he had been drinking.

Once indoors, Tom reverted to his usual habit of preparing sausage and chips. He lit the gas stove, set the chip pan on it, and then went into the living room to sit down while the chip fat heated. He fell asleep.

We don't know what woke him up. The kitchen had certainly caught fire. The noise of the flames or the smoke may have awakened his daughters upstairs, who, perhaps, began screaming. Maybe it was the noise of the flames that woke Tom up, or the sound of the fluorescent light in the kitchen, loosened by the heat, falling to the floor. Whatever it was, Tom's last action on earth was to open the kitchen door.

A fire investigator later reconstructed the scene. The chip pan fire in the small kitchen would have rapidly used up all the air in the small room. When Tom opened the door, and provided a fresh supply of oxygen, he was met by a literal ball of fire which would have suffocated and burned him to death in seconds.

That fireball caused a surge of flame into the upper part of the house, and effectively prevented one of Tom's neighbours saving his two daughters. The neighbour had noticed the glare of flames in the kitchen window and had run across the road to give help. He banged at the door and shouted, but got no response, and knowing that the

Tom had three pints at The Bell Inn, Appledore before embarking, with his children, on his last pub crawl.

two children would be sleeping upstairs, climbed on top of the porch to try to get into a bedroom. He could see that the room was full of dense smoke, but nevertheless was about to break through the window when the fireball that had killed Tom surged into the upper floor.

Almost at the same time, the fire brigade arrived. They found Lesley lying on the landing and Amanda on the floor beside her bed. Lesley died on the way to hospital. Amanda survived. I wonder how she will remember her father in the years to come?

14

To Die In Your Own Bed

Our current concern over drug abuse has, perhaps, made us forget the older and much less publicised problem of alcohol abuse, the consequences of which are just as distressing for the victim's relatives and just as humiliatingly harmful for the victims themselves.

Joanna Redwood was not that old when she died in bed in her sleep – 64 years – hadn't seen a doctor for the last five years, and her last evening alive had been spent listening to a play on Radio Four with a friend.

'She seemed very cheerful,' he told police later. 'She quite enjoyed the play. She was very happy.'

Well, we've all got to go sometime, and in bed, in your own home, with your children and grandchildren secure, is not a bad way to die, especially after a pleasant evening with a friend. In reality, Joanna Redwood's death was one of the most disgusting that I have encountered.

In her forties, she had been a comparatively wealthy woman, owning and managing a hotel with her husband. They had two daughters, and, in spite of the seven day a week demands of a hotel, the family was happy and united. Then the father died suddenly of cancer. Joanna could no longer run the hotel on her own, so sold it at a profit, moved into a quite expensive house, and began to live on the interest from her investments. She also began to drink. She was by no means a merry widow. She had loved her husband dearly, and her increasing reliance on drink was an attempt to blot out the sorrow of her loss.

Drink and teenage daughters began to make inroads on her investments. They moved to a smaller, but still quite comfortable, house. The drinking increased. Joanna was on the way to becoming a complete alcoholic. The daughters were now working, and not so dependent on her. When they expressed concern about her drinking, she ignored them. When they asked her about paying household bills, she accused them of trying to take control of her money. When they suggested that she needed help, advice, or counselling, she mocked them. They moved again. A yet smaller house in a poorer neighbourhood. The elder daughter, Alice, married and left home. Very soon, her sister came to her in a panic. Could she take her in until she found her own place? Mother was now drunk most of the time, the house saw a procession of her alcoholic friends, some of them almost vagrants.

The two daughters asked the family doctor to intervene. Joanna refused to see him. There was nothing he could do, other than refer the matter to the social services. Joanna refused to see them too, and moved again, this time to a two bedroomed terrace house. It was almost two years before Alice and her sister found where their mother had gone.

The house was an eyesore. The curtains at the windows were torn and filthy. Some of the windows were broken, and had clearly been broken for a long time. There was rubbish in the small garden. No one answered the door. The sisters knocked at a house across the street. They didn't say who they were.

'Oh, yes. Her. Drunk most of the time. Takes lodgers. Most of them as bad as her. Filthy woman. Council should do something about her. Plenty of money though. Often see her in the street with a couple of bottles of whiskey.'

The council, when the sisters had found the right

department, could do nothing about her. She had paid no council tax. Nor, apparently had she paid her electric, water or gas bills either. At some stage each of these services had been disconnected; each time a local charity, at the instigation of some unknown person, had paid for them to be reconnected.

They went back to the house. A half drunk Joanna answered the door to them. No, they couldn't come in. No, she didn't want to visit Alice and see her grandchildren. No, she wasn't all right, but why should they care. No one had ever cared for her, so they could just —— off.

A few months later they tried again. This time there was no answer. They heard dogs barking upstairs. The neighbour had not seen their mother for weeks.

'That lodger bloke, think his name's Charley, he's in and out. Mostly it's the off licence.'

The sisters went back to the social services. Well, if the mother would not let them in, there was little they could do, but they'd try again. This time they'd send a psychiatric social worker as well. It would be a week before they could get the appropriate staff.

When the social work team arrived at the house, they could get no answer. Officially they had no right to go in, but one of the ground floor windows was completely broken, so they stepped through that, found their way to the bedroom where Joanna lay dead, and called the police.

This is what the police found. There was no electricity, water, or gas connected to the house. The hall was two feet deep in rubbish, Paper, empty bottles, rotting food, human and canine faeces, and old clothing covered the floor from wall to wall. The downstairs kitchen was much the same. Empty bottles, cardboard boxes, bones, rotting food.

The two officers went outside to breath some fresh air, and then re-entered the house to go upstairs. In one room they could hear dogs barking and jumping against the door. The other room was Joanna's bedroom. Here, the rubbish was to the height of the bed, rotting food, empty bottles, faeces, filthy clothing. Joanna was lying on a double mattress without any covering. In places the springs had forced their way through; the only bed covering, an eiderdown, had rotted away into small pieces. A long wide hole had been cut or torn down the centre of the mattress. It had been there for a long time, and for a long time it had been used as a lavatory.

While the police were there, Charley appeared. Charley introduced himself as the lodger. He'd been out to buy whiskey. He told them about listening to the play on the radio the night before.

'She was happy,' he claimed, 'but I'm not surprised she's died. Hardly ate a thing.'

'How long have you lived here?'

'Me? Couple of years, I suppose. I've got my own room. I keep the dogs in there so they don't mess round the house.'

'Why haven't you tried to clear some of this rubbish away?' Even the landing on which the officer was talking to Charley was over a foot deep in trash.

'Couldn't do that,' said Charley. 'Got this bad back. Doctor told me not to lift anything.'

'So how long has the lady been ill?'

'She's been ill all the time I knew her.'

'What I meant was, how long has she been in bed?'

'In bed? Whit Sunday, it was, when she was last up. Hasn't moved out of that bed since.' Whit Sunday had been six months earlier. It was now the fifth of November.

The verdict was death from natural causes aggravated by self neglect.

15

In Peril From The Sea

There is a natural tendency amongst friends and relatives to look for someone to blame when a loved one has been killed. Someone must be at fault, and there are attempts at some inquests to get the Coroner to apportion that blame. When the Coroner fails to do so, he is often attacked for 'covering up for the establishment' or 'being a party to a whitewash'. I cannot stress too often that the Coroner's function is limited to finding out who died, how they died, and when or where they died. Blame is a matter for the civil or criminal courts.

Simon Kail set out one morning with his friend Rod Newburn to fish for mackerel. Rod owned a small open boat powered by an outboard motor, and was an experienced, albeit part-time, fisherman. He had a considerable local knowledge of the tides and weather, and was a strong swimmer. Simon could not swim, but the boat had four life jackets, a pair of oars in case the motor broke down, and six distress flares. On this September morning when they set out from Hartland Quay, the sea was calm, almost flat. They were fishing with rods, and intended to return around lunch time.

At midday the sea was slightly rougher, but far from dangerous, and the two men were wondering if they should turn back, have lunch and then come out again if the sea remained calm. Rod, glancing to the rear of the boat was astonished to see a huge wave coming towards them.

The sea was calm when Rod and Simon set out for a morning's fishing.

The wave lifted the stern of the boat and propelled it forward with the bow now pointing downwards at an angle. The speed of the wave forced the bow underwater and slowed down the boat's forward progress. In seconds the open boat was completely filled with water, and had overturned. The two men, each wearing a life jacket, were thrown into the sea, but were close enough to the now upside-down hull to be able to hold on for support. Two of the spare life jackets came to the surface and they were able to get hold of these, but it quickly became obvious that the boat was sinking.

There was no real panic. They were within sight of land, about three quarters of a mile from Hartland, the sea was still calm, the big wave had now disappeared, and their life jackets were easily keeping them afloat. They were, however, drifting out to sea. Rod, aware that Simon could not swim, attempted to teach him the basic arm and leg movements to help him to swim against the drift and get to shore. Simon was not satisfied that he would be able to swim, and suggested that Rod swam to the shore and got help while he stayed afloat using his own and one of the spare life jackets. It was comparatively warm, the sea was calm, and it would be easier for him to stay afloat and wait, rather than delay Rod who would be able to reach the shore much more quickly without him.

So Rod set off to swim the three quarters of a mile to the shore. It was noon when he started. By three o'clock, he was still half a mile from the shore, but still in sight of Simon who was now shouting for help to a small yacht. The yacht, which was never traced, apparently neither saw nor heard him. Rod continued to swim, but the currents had changed and six hours later he recognised the lights of Clovelly and hoped that he would be swept into the harbour there.

At about the same time, Rod's wife was becoming concerned about the absence of her husband. She knew that he had gone fishing with Simon in the morning, and she had been out for most of the day. When she came home in mid-afternoon, she presumed that Rod and Simon had been in for lunch, and gone out fishing again. But now it was dark, and Rod, she knew, was not equipped to be at sea in the dark. She had contacted Simon's parents but they were hoping that Simon was still with Rod. Perhaps they had had to go ashore at Clovelly because the tide had turned. But, the first thing they would have done would have been to phone her to let her know they were safe.

Hartland had until recently had its own coastguard station, but under the bitterly opposed reorganisation, the local coastguards were now controlled from their centre in Swansea. Mrs Newburn and Simon's parents went to the local hotel and dialled 999 – the emergency services in this part of the country include the coastguard – and were surprised to be put through to the centre at Falmouth. They knew enough of local conditions to know that the emergencies on that stretch of coast were dealt with by Swansea and Mrs Newburn told the Falmouth operator so. She was told to ring off and wait for a call from the Swansea centre.

Swansea rang her within five minutes. She told them of her fears and the possible location of her husband's boat. The control room, after generating a computer map of the area, directed a lifeboat there, as well as an air sea rescue helicopter, and a coastguard boat.

Meanwhile, the current had swept Rod away from Clovelly. He had to keep swimming to avoid becoming cold. At midnight he saw the lights of the rescue boats, shouted to them, and was hauled, almost unconscious from the water. The search for Simon continued, and his body was found by coastguards early in the morning only 400 yards from Hartland Point, from which the two friends had set out.

The only possible verdict was accidental death, but there were attempts to direct blame at the coastguards for the delay in finding Simon. In particular it was alleged that the computer-generated map had covered an area of 90 square miles, an unnecessarily wide area to search for a boat coming out from Hartland. There was also some local feeling that once Rod had been saved, it should have taken less time to locate Simon who might still have been alive.

'If we'd kept our own station here at Hartland, this would never have happened', was another local sentiment expressed in various parts of the media. The fact is that the coastguard centre at Swansea knew nothing of the two missing men until Mrs Newburn phoned them at 9.30 pm, and Rod, when he was pulled from the water, was too weak to give his rescuers any useful information.

The incident, coupled with another earlier drowning, formed the basis of a BBC documentary *In Peril On The Sea*, which was critical of the efficiency of the local coastguards.

In the earlier incident two 13 year old boys diving into the sea off rocks at Ilfracombe at the height of the holiday season got into difficulties when the sea became rougher than they thought it would be. Sam, who had dived in, found he was unable to get back onto the rocks; each time he reached them, he was swept back out by a wave. His friend Roger, a strong swimmer, dived in to help him. Almost at the same time, a particularly strong wave took hold of Sam and threw him onto the rocks. Roger could not regain the shore and was swept out to sea and drowned.

Their plight had not gone unnoticed. Holidaymakers on the nearby beach scrambled onto the rocks in an attempt to reach them. (Other holidaymakers stood by watching, some of them even videoing the event on camcorders.) The attendant at a nearby pitch and putt course phoned for help having seen the boys through his binoculars. This was at 4.15 pm. At 4.40 pm he phoned for help again as no one had arrived. As he was making his phone call, a coastguard vehicle arrived, and an air sea rescue helicopter appeared.

Within that quarter hour, a crowd of people had gathered, and there was a great deal of hostility towards the coastguards for their apparent delay. They were abused, and their vehicle kicked and thumped (this by people who had not thought to make use of the many lifebelts along the seafront at this point). The sea was still quite rough, and, more to demonstrate a willingness to do everything they could, rather than in any hope of being effective, one coastguard, secured by a rope, went into the sea with waves breaking over his head.

13 year old Roger was swept out to sea when he dived in to help a friend in difficulties.

The search was continued until dusk, and then abandoned until midnight when the low tide enabled a foot search to be made of the area. Roger's body was found some 20 yards from the beach, trapped in seaweed.

At the inquest, there was undisguised hostility towards the coastguards, who were represented by the controller from Swansea. His account was that the 4.15 pm message had only indicated that there were boys cut off by the tide, so the matter was not urgent, especially in the light of a number of hoax calls made that day, and another incident at another part of the coast. A PIW (person in water) message would have merited an instant response.

Following my verdict of accidental death, there were a number of approaches for me to reopen the inquest. Representatives for the relatives of the two boys had, quite properly, been able to obtain copies of the coastguard tapes relating to the first phone call. At the inquest, the pitch and putt attendant had not been absolutely sure that he had said that the boys were in the water. On the tapes, he had clearly said this at the end of a fairly long description of where the boys were. There was also a BT tape of another emergency call from a different phone which specifically spoke of boys being trapped by the tide.

My own feeling, and this is a personal rather than an official opinion, is that perhaps the operator who took the first message clearly did not know the area. Rapparee Cove is a difficult name to assimilate if you've never heard it before. Maybe the operator took down the first part of the emergency call paying more attention to the location than to the incident, and ignoring the caller's almost afterthought comment, that the boys were in the water.

16

The Winner

A surprising number of the unfortunates who commit suicide appear to have little, or no, reason for their act; a boy backs a tractor into his sister's car and within five minutes, hangs himself; a driver shoots himself at the scene of a very slight accident; a husband gases himself after his wife had mentioned that there was a very slight chance of her being made redundant. Sometimes there seems to be no reason at all.

G reg had been out at the pub for two hours at the most. He was not a heavy drinker, and his real objective was to meet a couple of other social club committee members to discuss the firm's annual summer outing. They'd only hired one coach, and Greg felt that if it was known that there were two coaches, a lot more people would put their names down. The other two were in full agreement with him. They'd get the rest of them working on it tomorrow.

Was Greg going to have another pint? No. Greg was going back home to Barbara.

After he'd left the others speculated on his relationship with his wife. 'Been married 25 years. Seem to get on well. No children.'

'Apparently they wanted kids, but they just never came. Some'd say they're better off.' They sipped their pints and went on to talk of other things.

Greg, in the meantime, had arrived home. Barbara wasn't a nagger. If he had stayed out drinking until midnight, she wouldn't have said anything. The next morning she might have asked where he had been, merely out of curiosity. No, Greg was home before ten because he wasn't a pub goer, and because he felt more comfortable with Barbara than with anyone else in the world. He unlocked the front door, called out Barbara's name, and noticed the envelope on the door mat.

He opened it. There was nothing in it other than a set of front door keys, Barbara's front door keys. There was a light on in the kitchen, and on the table a short note in Barbara's handwriting.

'All right. You've won. I've taken £100 and I'll let you have it back. I've put the keys through the front door. When I'm settled, I'll come back to collect my clothes.'

Greg sat down heavily at the kitchen table, reading and re-reading the note. It didn't make sense. What had he won? There'd been no argument of any sort. There was nothing that he was sticking out for against Barbara's wishes. When he left, she had been knitting in front of the telly.

'Won't be late,' he had said.

'I'll still be up,' she had smiled in reply.

'All right. You've won.' What did that mean? Was it some sort of joke? Greg went quickly through the other four rooms in the bungalow. She wasn't there. He began a more thorough search. There must be another note, something that would explain everything. After two hours of looking through drawers, searching through books, papers, boxes, he gave up. It was now midnight. If he rang her sister, or her friend Doris, they'd want to know what was going on if Barbara wasn't with either of them. Then when Barbara came back next day, she'd be embarrassed. Of course she would come back soon. Wasn't this a funny time of life for women, the fifties, when they went slightly off balance? She'd be back soon.

He sat up all night hoping to hear her knock at the door. Sometime in the early hours, he remembered that she had been knitting. She usually left her knitting on a special table in the corner of the room. It wasn't there. Had she gone out taking her knitting with her? He checked the coat rack in the hall again. All her coats were there. Had she gone out without a coat and with her knitting?

That was it. She had been called out to help a neighbour in a hurry. Someone in a car. She had taken her knitting because she knew she would be a long time, sitting by the bed of someone who was ill. That was it. The person was so ill that she hadn't wanted to use the phone because the sick person's family were waiting for the doctor, or a relative to ring, so the phone must not be engaged.

Greg felt enormous relief at solving the problem. Now he could get some sleep himself. It was going to be all right. Then he remembered the note. The sick person scenario had only been a way of avoiding the truth. Barbara had walked out. Why, he didn't know, but she had certainly gone.

The next day he didn't go into work. He phoned saying he was sick, getting off the phone as quickly as possible, so that Barbara could get through immediately. There were no calls. By the middle of the afternoon he had started ringing relatives and friends, admitting that Barbara was missing, hoping that one of them would have a clue to what she had done. He said nothing about the note, or about not taking clothes. No one knew anything. In the evening, Bill his neighbour called round.

'Better tell the police.'

There was something sinister about telling the police. Greg felt it would be admitting that something could have happened, or that Barbara could have done something terribly wrong, something completely out of character. But he and Bill went to the local station.

There was a young constable on duty who wanted to see the note.

'Well, she's not really missing, is she, sir? She's gone off of her own accord. That's plain from this note. Must have had a quarrel with her. Something you said, perhaps, that you took no notice of, something that she took exception to.'

Greg was visibly shocked. Why couldn't this officer understand that they had rarely quarrelled, certainly not that night. She had gone out without any extra clothes, not even a coat. She must be ill, wandering somewhere. If she wasn't found soon she'd catch pneumonia. The police must do something. An older PC, recognising Greg's real distress, took over. He entered Barbara's particulars into a register, and promised Greg that all the local hospitals would be contacted. As soon as they had any news they'd be in touch.

During the next two weeks, the police phoned Greg two or three times, and once came round to the house, but there was no news of Barbara. Greg went back to work. Bill, his neighbour asked him if he could borrow his step ladder to have a look in his gutters.

'Of course. Help yourself.' The step ladder was missing from the garage where it was usually kept. Clearly someone had stolen it. It didn't seem worthwhile reporting it to the police.

Then, at the end of the week, the maggots started appearing. On the Friday morning, before going out to work, he found them on the kitchen floor. He swept them up, sprinkled disinfectant on the floor and went out to work. When he returned in the evening, there were more in the same place.

'Must be a dead bird. Probably got trapped in the eaves. I'll sort it out in the morning.'

In the morning, there were more maggots, many more.

He had a pair of short steps. By putting these on the kitchen table, he could reach and open the door into the loft in the kitchen ceiling. There was no light in the loft, but he had a flashlight. With his feet on the steps and his body half into the loft, he shone the flashlight around. Very close to the loft door, he saw a blanket, and a pair of feet sticking out from one end.

He climbed down quickly, ran to tell Bill, and phoned for the police. Neither of them tried to go back into the loft. The two police officers found what was left of Barbara under the blanket, with several empty bottles of pills beside her. They also found the missing step ladder which she had used to get into the loft, and which she had pulled up behind her.

They also found Barbara's glasses, and her knitting, and a glass that had contained milk. The pathologist who examined her body estimated that she would have taken three or four hours to die. Death would have been painless, but there would be a point at which she realised that she was becoming sleepier and sleepier, and would soon be unconscious. It would have been at this point that she dropped the knitting which she had taken into the loft with her. Even assuming that she had climbed into the loft as soon as Greg had left the house, she would have been conscious, perhaps even still knitting, when Greg returned.

As he sat reading her note at the kitchen table, puzzling over her message about him winning, Barbara was knitting and waiting to die six feet above his head.

17

Nothing Changes

As you will have gathered, it is the responsibility of Her Majesty's Coroner to hold an enquiry into any violent, unnatural, or unexplained death that occurs in his area. It is almost the only responsibility left of all those that were attached to the office of Coroner when it was instituted in 1194, the year that Richard the Lionheart returned to England after years on the Crusades.

There's nothing new about this story. You've read it, or a version of it, more than once in your newspaper. Four men meet for a lunchtime drink in a South London pub. One of them, Chris, has a reputation for violence. He has already served time following a fight in which a man was killed. In the past twelve months, he has been bound over to keep the peace after another fight, and although he keeps quiet about it, he's waiting to go to court again. Chris is one of that strange breed of self-employed businessmen with interests in Europe, whom the intelligence services use for a spot of freelance spying.

But in spite of this rather dodgy background, or perhaps because of it, Chris is also a well known figure in London theatre circles. He's had a few minor roles, and a couple of his plays have been well liked both by critics and audiences. Two of the other men, Nick and Bob, are involved in part-time spying, while the fourth man, Ingram, has no connection with either the theatre or the intelligence services, and appears to have been a comparative newcomer to the others' company. Chris is openly gay, but there's no evidence that the meeting had any homosexual basis.

It's a warm pleasant day at the end of May, and the four men stay drinking and talking in the pub garden at the river's edge. There's no indication that they are other than on the best of terms. In the early evening, the quartet decide that they have enjoyed themselves so much that they'll stay at the pub for their evening meal. The single bar is now crowded with diners taking advantage of the warm evening, so the landlady clears one of her upstairs rooms in order that they can eat in comfort.

The meal ends, and the drinking continues. Almost inevitably at the end of such a day, when the bill comes to be paid, an argument breaks out – not between the guests and the landlady, but between Chris and Ingram. At first, it's no more perhaps than one drunk taking exception to some innocuous remark by another. Perhaps a suggestion that one had drunk and eaten twice as much as the other. Chris had been sprawled on a bed alongside the table, and Ingram was sitting with his back to him. It's not hard, in such circumstances, to imagine Chris mishearing or misinterpreting something that Ingram had said. Bob and Nick sitting at either side of the table were taking no part in the incipient quarrel, but in effect Ingram must have seen himself as surrounded by three men who knew each other very well, and who, in any potential quarrel, would act together against him.

At some point, Chris jumps up from the bed and, grabbing a knife from the back of Ingram's belt, slashes twice at Ingram's head. The latter, wounded and with blood streaming into his eyes, grabs the knife from Chris and in the ensuing struggle stabs him over the right eye. Chris dies almost immediately.

At the subsequent Coroner's inquest, the jury notes that

Ingram had made no attempt to escape after the killing, and finds that he had acted only in self defence.

As I said, it's a story that could turn up any weekend in any local newspaper. But the story is 400 years old. It is based on the report of Her Majesty's Coroner who, in 1593, held the inquest on the death of Christopher Marlowe, the author of *Dr Faustus* and *Tamburlane*.

The office of Coroner was set up in 1194 under the Articles of Eyre (the Eyre being the process under which the King's representatives visited each district in turn to hear criminal accusations). It was intended to ensure that the King received all the money due to him in civil and criminal matters, many of which related to death. The working rule appears to be that the sovereign owned everything unless someone else could prove it was theirs (a rule that still applies in cases of Treasure Trove), and the Coroner's real purpose was to guard the sovereign's interest. As the office was unpaid, Coroners added to their unpopularity by demanding fees for their duties. During the following 200 years the Coroner became one of the most unpopular of public figures, regarded by the people as no more than a tax gatherer.

The Articles never properly defined the role of the Coroner, and nearly all the legislation in the following 800 years that relates to the office has sought to curtail duties which Coroners took it upon themselves to exercise in the Middle Ages.

There is some evidence that the office existed in the time of Alfred the Great, but it was the 1194 Articles that created the *custos placitorum coronas* – the keepers of the pleas of the crown. Three knights were to be elected in each county. During the next two centuries, as the status of Coroner decreased, the requirement that he be a knight was dropped. As a result, the office became attractive to the upwardly mobile of medieval times and to those who saw it as a certain way of making money. In 1200, boroughs were also given a charter to elect their own Coroners, and in the next 100 years there were 256 Coroners in England and Wales. About 50 of these were Franchise Coroners, appointed by the King and nobles for their own enquiries. The Queen's Coroner, the Coroner for the Royal Household, and the Coroner for the Isles of Scilly are the only three surviving Franchise Coroners.

Then, as now, the Coroner's main concern was to enquire into violent or unnatural deaths (a common cause in medieval times seems to have been falling down a well whilst drunk), or into bodies found in the open. The 'first finder', or the person who first became aware of the body, was required to summon two to four neighbours who would in turn inform the sheriff, who called in the Coroner. The Coroner then held his enquiry into the cause of death. The body could not be moved until the Coroner had viewed it.

In one 12th century case, the first finder and his neighbours built a hedge around a body found in the open, knowing that the Coroner would not reach them for seven days. Such a delay was exceptional. Inquests were often held the day after the body had been found or the death notified to the Coroner.

At a time when travel was difficult and expensive, and when loss of a day's work was not compensated, it was not unknown for less scrupulous citizens to move a body found in their own area into a neighbouring hundred. The inquest required the attendance of the first finder, his four neighbours, a 'Presenter of Englishry' (i.e. someone who could testify that the deceased was English), and a jury of twelve men. In criminal matters, all these people might be required to travel later to the Eyre, where any subsequent criminal case would be heard. Imagine the disruption such a process would cause to an agricultural community.

It seems, then, that while the Coroner's primary role was to determine the cause of death, the function for which the office was really created was to impose fines on those who tried to avoid their duties in respect of the death. A Coroner could fine a person who discovered a body and did not report it. He could fine the neighbours who did not tell the sheriff. He could fine anyone who failed to attend the inquest and, later, anyone who failed to attend the Eyre. He could fine a whole community if these duties had not been carried out or had been avoided!

The Coroner's other financial role was to record the value of the goods belonging to criminals, potential criminals, and their victims, as these might eventually belong to the State. Until 1846, Coroners had the power to seize the objects which had caused death (the 'deodands'). In fact, this practice only stopped with the coming of the railways, when Coroners had to be prevented from seizing railway engines that had been involved in fatal accidents. Before this, others had exercised their doubtful powers to seize a barge from which a drunken sailor had fallen and drowned, a well into which a child had fallen, and the wheel of a wagon which had run over a traveller.

The duties and procedures that Coroners took upon themselves over the centuries were never envisaged in the Articles of 1194. They heard appeals – the medieval version of preferring a charge. They heard the evidence of the first 'supergrasses', convicted felons who turned 'approver' to escape punishment. They proclaimed as outlaws any accused who had failed to come to trial – an outlaw's goods, naturally, were forfeit to the crown – and fined any community in which the outlaw was known to have stayed. But none of their appointed, or self assumed, responsibilities can have been as futile as the farce of overseeing the ritual known as 'abjuring the realm'.

'Abjuring the realm' was an option available to criminals accused of a serious crime such as murder, rape or robbery during the 12th and 13th centuries. First they had to escape the 'hue and cry', a pursuit by a posse raised in the vicinity of the crime. This was more than just good citizenship on the part of the local inhabitants; a community which failed to raise a hue and cry could, you will not be surprised to learn, be fined. However, a pursued criminal could obtain sanctuary for a limited period of 40 days in a monastery, church or chapel, and any adjoining graveyard. Until that time expired, no one had the authority to remove him.

At the end of the 40 days, the felon left the church, confessed his guilt to the Coroner, and offered to leave the country, or 'abjure the realm'. It was the Coroner's responsibility to hand him a wooden cross, dress him in sackcloth, and direct him to a port from which he should leave. The Coroner also had to lead him to the road he would have to take, one of the conditions being that the felon did not leave that road before arriving at the port.

The penalty for an abjurer leaving the appointed road was summary execution by hanging or beheading. Many criminals must have been pulled from the road by their enemies and killed, the latter then claiming that their victim had left the road. In fact, there were a number of hitches in what, at first sight, was a straightforward process, and everyone concerned with the system probably knew how to exploit its shortcomings. Naturally the crown had a financial interest. Any community which allowed the felon, easily recognisable by his cross and sackcloth, to leave the road, was fined.

By the time of Magna Carta in 1215, Coroners had decided that their role also included hearing pleas of the crown – in effect, the trying of criminal cases. Magna Carta made it clear they had no right to do so, but medieval Coroners had less respect for that document than we might suppose, and many continued in their judge-like role.

By the end of the 14th century, the Eyre had fallen into misuse, and the offices of escheator and justice of the peace had been established. The escheator took over the responsibility of deciding the value of a criminal's or victim's goods, and the justices heard pleas. It seems as if the office of justice of the peace was instituted to exercise some control over Coroners!

Until 1487, Coroners were unpaid, the assumption being that they would carry out their duties voluntarily, like good middle class citizens. However, Coroners seem to have adopted the habit of charging to hold an inquest – although in theory they could be taxed if they failed to hold one. Pity the poor citizen who faced a choice between a fine if they failed to tell the Coroner about a death, and paying the Coroner to carry out his duty! Possibly the worst known case is that of a Sussex woman who drowned and whose body lay unburied for nine weeks until the Coroner was finally paid and agreed to hold the inquest. Coroners had also initiated the custom of confiscating for their own use the jacket or upper garment of any corpse upon which they held an inquest.

There were other malpractices, including issuing false appeals so as to extort money from defendants. On the other hand, it must be said that there was a great deal of deliberate obstruction of the Coroner in his duty, with clerics, nobles and landowners often preventing the holding of inquests in order to seize the goods of the deceased for themselves.

The 1487 Recognisance Act introduced a set fee for every inquest, accompanied by a hefty fine for any Coroner who failed to hold an inquest, and by 1500 the Coroner's role had effectively been limited to holding inquests into violent deaths. However, the paying of a fee seems to have spurred some Coroners to hold unnecessary inquests, and in 1509 another Act forbade them to hold inquests on deaths from misadventure. Over 200 years later, when fees were increased and travelling expenses introduced, it was clear that Coroners were still unnecessarily investigating sudden deaths, and justices were ordered to curtail this practice by withholding fees.

Even as late as 1836, the Births and Deaths Registration Act was still attempting, among other matters, to stop Coroners holding unnecessary inquests and claiming the fees. To be fair to the Coroners of that time, however, it is believed that murders were going undetected because of the artificial limitations on the type of death that might attract a Coroner's interest.

In 1860, a House of Commons committee recommended that Coroners be put on a salaried rather than a fee basis. Their remit was extended to hold inquests into violent deaths, unnatural deaths, sudden and unexplained deaths, and any deaths suspected to have been caused by criminal action.

The subsequent 1887 Coroners Act became the basis of the modern service, giving Coroners their current responsibilities of inquiring into sudden, violent and unexplained deaths and into Treasure Trove. In 1926, the Coroners Amendment Act required Coroners to be informed of every uncertificated death, giving them the right to decide whether or not there should be an inquest. In 1961, suicide was decriminalised, but it remained an offence for anyone to assist in a suicide. Coroners' juries could still commit witnesses for trial for such an offence until 1977, when the right of the jury to commit someone for trial for murder or manslaughter was removed, and the need to summon a jury was limited. In 1980, the 800 year old requirement that a Coroner should physically view the body was ended.

119

A Coroner is still, today, a servant of the Crown, and by tradition ranks next to the Sheriff in any county ceremony. In many recent cases, as you will have gathered, it has been clear that the media and the general public, as well as individuals with a proper interest in the death, expect the Coroner to apportion blame, to decide guilt, to condemn inefficiency, corruption and brutality, and to avenge injustice. One hundred years ago, Coroners might have taken on any or all of these roles. Today, their responsibility is only to record who has died, and how, when and where the death occurred.Their role is unique in our legal system in that an inquest is a process of ascertaining the truth about these limited facts.

18

The Coroner's Officer

Keith James, a former police sergeant, was my Coroner's Officer for nine years. His responsibilities included attending all scenes of sudden death, informing me of those in which the Coroner has an interest, interviewing, or arranging for the interviewing of, all relevant witnesses, and liaising with me on the subsequent inquest. In fact, he did most of the work, so it's fitting that he should tell you about himself before we finish.

I saw my first dead body when I was still a police cadet. A boy had jumped off the bridge at Barnstaple at high tide, and about four hours later, one of the local fishermen had snagged the body in his net. The bobby on that beat was having his lunch, so I was sent out from the police station to give whatever assistance a callow 17 year old could give to an old Devon fisherman.

When I got there, the fisherman was sitting patiently in his boat holding the poor boy's body out of the water by the hair, watched by a crowd then about five deep on the bridge above him. Another fisherman rowed me out to him. There was nothing in any of the police regulations that I knew about dealing with dead bodies, but we could obviously not just sit in the middle of the river waiting for a more experienced bobby to arrive, so I helped the fisherman to pull the body into the boat, covered it with my tunic, and told him to row back to the shore. I had no idea what would happen when I got there, and I concentrated on not looking at the boy's face; his eyes and ears had already been eaten by fish.

Knowing the reluctance of the local bobby to hurry anywhere, especially when he was in the middle of his refreshment break, I was quite surprised to find him waiting for us when we got back to the river's edge. When he had heard about the death, he used the commonsense that all old policemen develop and phoned the appointed undertaker, getting the latter to pick him up from the station before driving him down to the bridge.

'You leave it all to me now, boy. Better get back to the station,' he told me, speaking more kindly and patiently than I had come to expect from my older colleagues, before he, the undertaker, and the fisherman began to move the body into the back of the undertaker's hearse.

It was a few days before I realised the reason for his patience. In those days, a sudden death was a bonus for a policeman. He automatically became the Coroner's Officer for that death for which he was paid 3/6d, or about 16p in today's money, or half a day's wages then. He would be paid another 3/6d for arranging the inquest, and when a jury was needed, a further 3/6d for summoning a jury. In addition, he was relieved of all other duties until the inquest was over.

The last death I attended as a police officer, just before I took on this job, was that of an old gentleman who had died watching television and had been found sitting in front of the screen by his son, who had called the police.

When I arrived, the body was still sitting in front of the set, but the son had preserved the decencies by covering it with a sheet. He told me what had happened.

'I switched the set off,' he said, hesitantly. 'Do you reckon that was the right thing to do?' I assured him that it was the right thing to do. He looked relieved.

'I expect you'd like to see Father,' he suggested. When

Keith James.

I indicated that I thought this was a good idea, he pulled back the sheet, and I satisfied myself that Father, still dressed in his shirt and tie, and looking very peaceful, was indeed dead.

The doctor had already been to the house, and had certified death, so there was nothing more for me to do, other than arrange for the Coroner's undertaker to attend to remove the body, but Frank, the son, seemed reluctant for me to go.

'I'm waiting for the rest of the family to come round. If you were here when they came, it would be a bit more official.' So I agreed to stay. Frank made a cup of tea, and we had a polite conversation while Father sat unmoving in front of the TV. There was a knock on the door. Brother number two came in. I was introduced. Father was unveiled. Number two brother nodded his satisfaction. We all had another cup of tea, and when the third brother arrived, I considered that I had done as much as anyone could expect. The sheet was pulled back, more tea was poured, and the state of the garden was discussed yet again. I marked the end of my official visit by tying an identification label to the old man's wrist. Rigor mortis was setting in, and it was a bit difficult to get Father's arm back under the sheet.

'For goodness' sake, Father, sit still while the policeman does his job,' muttered Frank before he realised what he was saying. Well, to save his embarrassment I agreed to stay for another cup of tea until sister came.

'Her got a bit further to come,' Frank confided.

Sister came. Everything was quiet as she came in. The tea cups were put carefully down. Frank had not been able to warn her in advance; this was her regular morning visit. He kept her in the hall to tell her what had happened. Luckily there were no tears, no screams. She was ushered into the front room, introduced to me – ' Sergeant James is looking after everything' – and invited to look at Father. The sheet was moved back. Father was still there, still peaceful.

'What a shame,' she said, finally. 'I've brought him a nice duck for his dinner. He will be sorry to have missed it.' It was time for me to go. I don't know who got the duck.

I've found it very important to let relatives talk all they can about a death. Quite often, at the end of such conversations, you feel able to say, 'She sounded a really nice old lady' or 'What a mean old beggar he was', and be sure that the relatives will agree with you. They don't realise how clearly their own feelings have come across, and sometimes, for a moment, believe that you must have known the dead person as well as they did.

One corpse I particularly remember was that of a very well groomed man of about 85. Even in death he seemed to have a smile on his face. I mentioned this to his son, who was glad of the opportunity to speak about a father whom he clearly loved.

'He had a good innings. The family always had Christmas dinner together. Every year after dinner, when the port went round, he'd raise his glass in a toast to all of us and say "I won't be here next year to have this drink with you." Of course, we said it was nonsense, and that he'd see us all out. Anyway, when he died, he'd left his will in a drawer in his desk. When we took it out, a little piece of paper dropped out. It was a note saying "Told you I wouldn't be here next year".'

I get very occasional requests to arrange unusual burials. If you want to bury someone in his or her own garden you need planning permission from the local authority. You also need a certificate from the National Rivers Authority to show that the intended grave does not fall on a water line or water source. There must also be at least three foot of bedrock below the coffin. Perhaps the real deterrent to such burials is the requirement that the location of the grave be shown on the deeds of the house. I understand it reduces the value of the property by about 50 per cent.

Sea burials are even more difficult. There are only two places off the south coast where sea burials are permitted, and there is a mass of regulations covering the construction of the coffin. I did once have a request for a sea burial off Lynmouth. I told the caller that this would not be allowed, but he persisted. He said he knew of someone who had been buried off Lynmouth, and he could not understand why I was making difficulties. I told him that I had been working here for the last twelve years and had never heard of such a burial. No, he wasn't satisfied.

It was one of those occasions when I had to judge the mood of the person at the other end of the phone. Well, yes, I admitted. There had been one sea burial at Lynmouth.

'There you are,' he said. 'So what's the problem?'

'The problem was that we had to bury him 28 times. He kept coming back on shore. In the end we had to put him in an ordinary grave.'

There was a long silence, then he burst into howls of laughter and rang off. I never heard from him again.

But, going back to relatives and the inquest, I think it most important to maintain this position of a family friend. You are dealing with people who may never have been in any court at all in their lives. They are apprehensive and stressed. I try to put them at their ease by emphasising the informality of the proceedings.

'It's nothing like Rumpole of the Bailey,' I tell them. This invariably breaks the ice, and makes it easier for them to deal with any trauma caused by the proceedings. It is not making little of their sorrow to say that most people leave the court with a smile on their face. All the formality connected with the death is over. The State has finished with them, and mourning, celebration, or recollection are now matters only for the family. If the Coroner's Officer has done his job well, the relatives will have been treated with respect and good humour, and they will know that there is someone at the end of the phone who is always willing to answer their questions even years after the death.

I'm sometimes asked to suggest an epitaph. My favourite is:

> 'Grieve not that I have died.
> Rejoice that I have lived.'

Index